D1486465

Returning to Reims

Returning to Reims

Didier Eribon

Translated by Michael Lucey

ALLEN LANE
an imprint of
PENGUIN BOOKS

ALLEN LANE

UK | USA | Canada | Ireland | Australia
India | New Zealand | South Africa

Penguin Books is part of the Penguin Random House group of companies
whose addresses can be found at global.penguinrandomhouse.com.

First published as *Retour à Reims* 2009
This translation first published by Semiotext(e) 2013
Published by Allen Lane 2018
001

Printed in Great Britain by Clays Ltd, St Ives plc

A CIP catalogue record for this book is available from the British Library

ISBN: 978–0–241–34462–0

www.greenpenguin.co.uk

Penguin Random House is committed to a
sustainable future for our business, our readers
and our planet. This book is made from Forest
Stewardship Council® certified paper.

For G., who always wants to know everything.

1

FOR THE LONGEST TIME it was nothing more than a name to me. My parents had moved to the village in question at a point in time when I no longer went to see them. From time to time, while traveling abroad, I would send them a postcard, all that remained of an effort to sustain a connection that for my part I wished as tenuous as possible. While writing their address, I might briefly wonder what the place where they now lived was like, but my curiosity went no further than that. On those rare occasions when I spoke to my mother on the telephone—perhaps once or twice every few months, perhaps less—she would ask me, "When are you coming to visit?" I would give a vague answer, mentioning how busy I was, promising to come soon. But I had no intention of doing so. I had left my family behind and had no desire to return to it.

So it was only quite recently that I came to know Muizon. It was pretty much as I had expected: a typical instance of a certain kind of "rurbanization," one of those semi-urban spaces built out in the middle of the fields, where it is difficult to tell if it is still part of the countryside or if, with the passage of time, it has become something like a suburb. At the beginning of the 1950s, I have since learned, it had no more than 50 inhabitants. They were clustered together around a church, parts of which dated to the twelfth century, having survived the devastation due to the endless stream of wars that has washed over the northeast of France, a region with, in Claude Simon's words, "a particular status," where names of towns and villages seem synonymous with "battles" or "armed camps" or "muffled cannon fire" or "vast cemeteries."[1] These days more than two thousand people live in Muizon, between, on the one side, the Route du Champagne, which begins quite close by to wind its way through vine-covered hillsides, and, on the other, a grim-looking industrial zone, part of the outskirts of Reims, which is about a fifteen or twenty minute car ride away. New streets have been laid down, lined with identical houses, built in groups of two. Most of these are public housing; their tenants are far from rich. My parents lived there for twenty years without me ever making up my mind to go see them. I finally found myself in this municipality—I'm not sure exactly how to refer to a place like this—and inside my parents' small house only after my father had left it, my mother having found him a place in a nursing facility for Alzheimer's patients, where he would reside until his death. She had put off the inevitable moment as long as possible, until finally, worn out and frightened (one day he had grabbed a kitchen knife and attacked her), she gave in to what had become increasingly obvious: she had no other options. It was only once he was no longer in the house that it became possible for me to undertake this return voyage, or maybe I should say, to begin the process of returning, something I had never been able to make up my mind to do before. It was a rediscovery of that "region of myself," as Genet would have said, from which I had worked so hard to escape: a social space I had kept at a distance, a mental space in opposition to which I had constructed the person I had become, and yet which remained an essential part of my being. So I returned to see my mother and this turned out to be the beginning of a reconciliation with her. Or, to be more precise, it began a process of reconciliation with myself, with an entire part of myself that I had refused, rejected, denied.

My mother spoke with me at great length during the several visits I made in the course of the next few months. She spoke of herself, of her childhood, her adolescence, her life as a married woman... She also spoke to me about my father, how they met, what their relationship was like, of the different periods in their lives, the harshness of the jobs they had worked in. She had so much to tell me that her words tumbled out rapidly in an endless stream. She seemed intent on making up for lost time, erasing in one swoop all the sadness represented for her by those many conversations between us that had never happened. I would listen, seated across from her, drinking my coffee, attentive when she was talking about herself, much less so when she got caught up in describing the doings of her grandchildren, my nephews, whom I had never met, and in whom I wasn't much interested. Between the two of us a relationship was being reestablished. Something in me was being repaired. I could also see how difficult the distance I had kept had been for her to deal with. I understood that she had suffered from it. How had it been for me, the person responsible for it? Had I not also suffered, but in a different way, one delineated in the Freudian vision of "melancholy," associated with an unavoidable mourning of the various possibilities one sets aside, the various identifications one rejects? Such possibilities and such identifications remain in the self as one of its constitutive elements. Whatever you have uprooted yourself from or been uprooted from still endures as an integral part of who or what you are. Perhaps a sociological vocabulary would do a better job than a psychoanalytic one of describing what the metaphors of mourning and of melancholy allows one to evoke in terms that are simple, but also misleading and inadequate: how the traces of what you were as a child, the manner in which you were socialized, persist even when the conditions in which you live as an adult have changed, even when you have worked so hard to keep that past at a distance. And so, when you return to the environment from which you came—which you left behind—you are somehow turning back upon yourself, returning to yourself, rediscovering an earlier self that has been both preserved and denied. Suddenly, in circumstances like these, there rises to the surface of your consciousness everything from which you imagined you had freed yourself and yet which you cannot not recognize as part of the structure of your personality—specifically the discomfort that results from belonging to two different worlds, worlds so far separated from each other that they seem irreconcilable, and yet which coexist in everything that you are. This is a melancholy related to a "split *habitus*," to invoke Bourdieu's wonderful, powerful concept. Strangely enough, it is precisely at the moment in which you try to get past this diffuse and hidden kind of malaise, to get over it, or when you try at least to allay it a bit, that it pushes even more strongly to the fore, and that the melancholy associated with it redoubles its force. The feelings involved have always been there, a fact that you discover or rediscover at this key moment; they were lurking deep inside, doing their work, working on you. Is it ever possible to overcome this malaise, to assuage this melancholy?

When I telephoned my mother a little after midnight on December 31 that year to wish her a happy new year, she announced: "The nursing home just called me. Your father died an hour ago." I didn't love him. I never had. I had known that he only had months, and then days, to live, and yet I had made no effort to see him one last time. What would have been the point, really, since he wouldn't have recognized me? It had, in any case, been years since either of us had really recognized the other. The gap that had begun to separate us when I was a teenager had only grown wider with the passage of time, to the point where we were basically strangers. There was nothing between us, nothing that held us together. At least that is what I believed, or struggled to believe; it had been my idea that one could live one's life separate from one's family, reinventing oneself and turning one's back on the past and the people in it.

At the time, it seemed to me that for my mother his death was a kind of liberation. My father had been sinking more and more deeply day by day into a state of physical and mental decay, and it could only get worse. It was an inexorable process. There was no chance of a cure. He alternated between periods of dementia during which he fought with his nurses, and long periods of torpor, doubtless due in part to the drugs he was given when he became agitated. During these subdued periods he would not speak or walk or eat. In any case, he remembered nothing and no one. His sisters found it enormously difficult to visit him (two of them were too frightened to return after their first visit), as did my three brothers. As for my mother, who had to drive twenty kilometers to the nursing home, her devotion astonished me. It was astonishing because I knew that her feelings for him were—and, for as long as I can remember had always been—made up of a mixture of hatred and disgust. I am not exaggerating: hatred and disgust. Yet for her, this was a duty. It was her own image of herself that was at stake. "I can't just leave him there all alone," she would repeat each time I asked her why she made a point of visiting the nursing home every day, even after he no longer knew who she was. She had put up on the door of his room a photograph of the two of them together and pointed it out to him regularly. "Do you know who that is?" He would reply, "It's the lady who takes care of me."

Two or three years earlier, the news of my father's condition had provoked in me a huge attack of anxiety. Not really so much for him—it was too late and, in any case, I felt very little towards him, not even compassion. Rather, selfishly, I was worried about myself. Was this a hereditary condition? Would it soon be my turn? I set myself to reciting all the poems or scenes from classical tragedy that I had learned by heart to see if I still knew them: "Songe, songe, Céphise, à cette nuit cruelle qui fut pour tout un peuple une nuit éternelle…";[2] "Voici des fruits, des fleurs, des feuilles et des branches/ Et puis voici mon coeur…";[3] "L'espace à soi pareil, qu'il s'accroisse ou se nie/Roule dans cet ennui…".[4] No sooner would I forget a line than I would tell myself, "It's started." I have yet to rid myself of this obsession. As soon as my memory stumbles over a name or a date or a telephone number, I become uneasy. I see warning signs everywhere: I seek them out and I fear them in equal measure. There is a way in which my daily life is now haunted by Alzheimer's—a ghost arriving from the past in order to frighten me by showing me what is still to come. In this way, my father remains present in my existence. It seems a strange way indeed for someone who has died to survive within the brain—the very place in which the threat is located—of one of his sons. Lacan writes remarkably in one of his *Seminars* of this door that opens onto anxiety for children, or at least for sons, at the moment of their father's death, for then the son finds himself on the front lines facing death alone. Alzheimer's adds a more ordinary, day-to-day kind of fear to this ontological anxiety: you are always on the lookout for symptoms, ready to turn them into a diagnosis.

Yet my life is not only haunted by the future; there are also the ghosts of my own past, ghosts which leapt into view immediately upon the death of the person who incarnated everything I wanted to run away from, everything I wanted to break with. My father certainly constituted for me a kind of negative social model, a reference point against which I had performed all the work I undertook as I struggled to create myself. In the days that followed his death, I set to thinking about my childhood, about my adolescence, about all the reasons that had led me to hate the man who had just died and whose end, along with the unexpected emotions it provoked in me, woke in my memory so many different images I had believed forgotten. (Or perhaps I had known on some level that I hadn't forgotten them, even if I had made an effort, a quite conscious one, to repress them.) Some people might remark that this is something that happens during any period of mourning. It might even be said to be a universal feature of mourning, an essential characteristic of it, especially when it is parents who are being mourned. Even if that is the case, I had a strange way of experiencing it: a kind of mourning in which the urge to understand something about the person who had passed away and something about the person—myself—who has survived predominates over any sadness. Other losses, earlier ones, had affected me more deeply and caused me much deeper distress—the loss of friends, of people I had made the choice to be involved with, people whose sudden disappearance ripped something from the fabric of my daily life. Unlike these relationships I had chosen, whose strength and stability came from the fact that the parties involved ardently desired to perpetuate them (a feature which explains the feeling of dejection that occurs when they are cut off), my relationship with my father seemed to me to be only a biological and a legal one: he had fathered me, and I bore his name, but other than that he didn't much matter to me. Reading the notes in which Roland Barthes kept a daily record of the despair that enveloped him when his mother died, of the unbearable suffering that then transformed his life, I am struck by the degree to which the feelings that took hold of me when my father died differ from his despair and affliction. "I'm not mourning, I'm suffering," he writes as a way of expressing his refusal of a psychoanalytic approach to understanding what happens after the death of a loved one.[5] What was happening to me? Like Barthes, I could say that I was not "in mourning" (in the Freudian sense of working through something in a psychic temporality where the initial pain gradually lessens). But nor was I experiencing an indelible suffering on which time could have no effect. What, then, was going on? A state of confusion and disarray, perhaps, produced by something being called into question, something both personal and political, something about one's social destiny, about the way society is divided into classes, about the role played by a number of different social determinants in the constitution of individual subjectivities, something to do with individual psychologies, with the relations that exist between individuals.

I did not attend my father's funeral. I had no desire to see my brothers again, having been out of touch with them for thirty years. All I knew of them was what I could see in the framed photographs found all around the house in Muizon. So I knew what they looked like, how they had changed physically over the years. But what would it have been like to meet them again in these particular circumstances? "How he has changed," we would all have been thinking about each other, desperately seeking in our appearance today the signs of what we looked like a while back, a good while back, when we were brothers, when we were young. The day after the funeral, I went and spent the afternoon with my mother. We spent a few hours chatting, seated in the armchairs in her living room. She had brought out from a cupboard some boxes filled with photographs. There were pictures of me, of course, as a young boy and a teenager—and of my brothers. There it was in front of my eyes again (but wasn't it in fact still inscribed in my mind and in my flesh?), that working class environment I had grown up in, the incredible poverty that is palpable in the appearance of all the houses in the background, in the interiors, in the clothes everyone is wearing, in the very bodies themselves. It is always startling to see to what an extent bodies in photographs from the past (and perhaps this is even more the case than for bodies we see in action or in situation in front of us) appear before our eyes as social bodies, bodies of a certain class. It can be equally startling to remark to what extent a photograph, a "souvenir," by returning an individual—in this case, me—to his or her familial past, ties that person to his or her social past. The private sphere in even its most intimate manifestations, when it resurfaces in old snapshots, can still serve to reinscribe us in the very particular social location from which we came, in places marked by class, in a topography in which that which you might take as belonging to the most fundamentally personal kinds of relations nonetheless plants you firmly in a collective history, a collective geography. (It is as if tracing any individual genealogy were somehow inseparable from uncovering a social archaeology, a social topology that is there in each of us, one of our most fundamental truths, even if not one of the ones we are most aware of.)

2

THERE WAS A QUESTION that had begun to trouble me a bit earlier, once I had taken the first steps on this return journey to Reims. I would manage to formulate it still more clearly and more precisely in the days that followed the afternoon of the day after my father's funeral, the one I spent with my mother going through old photographs: "Why, when I have written so much about processes of domination, have I never written about forms of domination based on class?" Or, "Why, when I have paid so much attention to the role played by feelings of shame in processes of subjection and subjectivation, have I written so little about forms of shame having to do with class?" Finally, it came to seem necessary to me to pose the question in these terms: "Why, when I have had such an intense experience of forms of shame related to class, shame in relation to the milieu in which I grew up, why, when once I had arrived in Paris and started meeting people from such different class backgrounds I would often find myself lying to them about my class origins, or feeling embarrassed when admitting my background in front of them, why had it never occurred to me to take up this problem in a book or an article?" Let me put it this way: it turned out to be much easier for me to write about shame linked to sexuality than about shame linked to class. It seemed that the idea of studying the constitution of subordinated subjectivities, and, simultaneously, the establishment of a complicated relationship between remaining silent about oneself and making an "avowal" of who one is, had become these days valorized and valorizing, that it was even strongly encouraged in the contemporary political context— when it was sexuality that was in question. Yet the same kind of project was extremely difficult, and received no support from prevailing categories of social discourse, when it was a question of working-class social origins. I wanted to understand why this would be the case. Fleeing to the big city, to the capital, in order to be able to live out one's homosexuality is such a classic trajectory, quite common for young gay men. The chapter that I wrote on this phenomenon in *Insult and the Making of the Gay Self* can be read—as, in fact, the whole first section of that book can be— as an autobiography recast as historical and theoretical analysis, or, if you prefer, as a historical and theoretical analysis that is grounded in personal experience.[6] But the "autobiography" in question was a partial one. A different historical and theoretical analysis would also have been possible beginning with a similarly reflexive look at the path I had followed. This is because the decision at the age of twenty to leave the town in which I was born and where I spent my adolescence in order to go live in Paris also represented part of a progressive change in my social milieu. On thinking the matter through, it doesn't seem exaggerated to assert that my coming out of the sexual closet, my desire to assume and assert my homosexuality, coincided within my personal trajectory with my shutting myself up inside what I might call a class closet. I mean by this that I took on the constraints imposed by a different kind of dissimulation; I took on a different kind of dissociative personality or double consciousness (with the same kinds of mechanisms familiar from the sexual closet: various subterfuges to cover one's tracks, a very small set of friends who know the truth but keep it secret, the taking up of different registers of discourse in different situations and with different interlocutors, a constant self-surveillance as regards one's gestures, one's intonation, manners of speech, so that nothing untoward slips out, so that one never betrays oneself, and so on). When, after writing a number of books dealing with the history of ideas (including my two books on Foucault), I began the project of writing about subjection, it was on my gay past that I chose to draw. I chose to reflect on the workings of subordination and "abjection" (how a person is "abjected" by the surrounding world) experienced by those of us who contravene the laws of sexual normality, thereby leaving aside everything in me, in my own existence, that could—and should—have led me to turn my gaze on relations of class, to class domination, to the processes of subjectivation linked to class affiliation and to the subordination of the working classes. Of course it's not as if I totally neglected these questions in *Insult and the Making of the Gay Self*, or in *Une morale du minoritaire* [A minoritarian morality] or in *Hérésies*.[7] My ambition in these books was larger than the specific framework of the analyses found in them. I wanted to sketch out an anthropology of shame and from it to build up a theory of domination and of resistance, of subjection and subjectivation. Surely that is why, in *Une morale du minoritaire*, I kept juxtaposing the theoretical elaborations of Genet, Jouhandeau, and several other writers who deal with sexual subordination with the thinking of Bourdieu on class subordination or of Fanon, Baldwin, and Chamoiseau on racial and colonial subordination. Yet it remains the case that these dimensions are only dealt with in the course of my demonstration as other parameters that contribute to an effort to understand what the fact of belonging to a sexual minority represents and carries along with it. I call on approaches produced in other contexts; I make an effort to extend the range of my analyses; but these other approaches remain a bit secondary. They are supplements—sometimes offering support, sometimes suggesting ways of extending my analysis. As I pointed out in the preface to *Insult and the Making of the Gay Self*, I wanted to transpose the notion of a class *habitus* developed by Pierre Bourdieu to the question of sexual *habitus*: do the forms of incorporation of the structures of the sexual order produce sexual *habitus* in the same way that the forms of incorporation of the structures of the social order produce class *habitus*? And even though any attempt to develop a response to a problem like this one must obviously confront the question of the articulation between sexual *habitus* and class *habitus*, my book was devoted to sexual subjectivation and not social or class subjectivation.

When I returned to Reims, I was confronted by the following question, a tenacious one I had not acknowledged (at least I had not really acknowledged it in my written work, or in my life): in taking as my point of theoretical departure—by which I mean establishing a framework for thinking about myself, my past, and my present—the seemingly obvious idea that the complete break I had made with my family was due to my homosexuality, to my father's deeply rooted homophobia, to the homophobia rampant in the milieu in which I was living (and doubtless all this was absolutely true), had I not at the same time offered myself noble and incontestable reasons for avoiding the thought that this was just as much a break with the class background I came from?

In the course of my life, following the typical path of a young gay man who moves to the city, builds up new social networks, and learns what it means to be gay by discovering the gay world that already exists, inventing himself as gay on the basis of that discovery, I had also followed another path, a class-based one: this is the itinerary of those who are frequently labeled "class traitors." And surely a "traitor" or a "renegade" is what I was, one whose only concern, a more or less permanent and more or less conscious one, was to put as much distance as possible between himself and his class of origin, to escape from the social surroundings of his childhood and his adolescence.[8]

Of course I retained a political solidarity with the world of my early years, to the extent that I never came to share the values of the dominant class. I always felt awkward or incensed when hearing people around me talking scornfully or flippantly about working class people and their habits and ways of life. After all, that's where I came from. I would also experience an immediate hatred on encountering the hostility that well-to-do, well-established people would express towards strikes, political activism, protests, and forms of popular resistance. Certain class reflexes persist despite all our efforts to separate ourselves from our social origins, even those efforts aimed at personal transformation. And on those occasions in my daily life, rare but not non-existent,

in which I gave way to hasty and disdainful opinions that charac-
terize a view of the world and other people that we might as well
call class racism, my reactions nonetheless more often than not
resembled those of Paul Nizan's character, Antoine Bloyé. A portrait of Nizan's father, Bloyé is a former worker who has become
bourgeois, and he still feels hurt by the derogatory remarks about
the working class that he hears made by those people around
him who now constitute his social milieu. It feels as if he were
being targeted along with the milieu to which he used to belong:
"How could he share their opinions without completely betraying
his own childhood?"[9] Every time I would "betray" my own childhood, by sharing in deprecatory opinions, inevitably a nagging
bad conscience would make itself felt, if not sooner, then later.

And yet, an enormous distance seemed to separate me now
from the universe I had once belonged to, a universe that I had
devoted so much energy—the energy of despair—to breaking
with. I have to admit that however much I felt close to and in
solidarity with working class struggles, however loyal I
remained to those political and emotional values that are stirred
in me whenever I watch a documentary about the great strikes
of 1936 or 1968, still, deep inside myself I experienced a rejection of working class life as I knew it. The "organized" working
class, or the working class perceived as organizable, and thereby
idealized, even rendered heroic, is different from the individuals
from whom it is made up, or who potentially make it up. And
it became more and more unpleasant for me to find myself in
the company of those who were—of those who are—members
of this class. In my early days in Paris, when I still visited my

parents, who were still living in the same public housing project in Reims where I had spent my adolescence (it was only many years later that they would move from there to Muizon), or when I had lunch with them on Sundays at my grandmother's, who lived in Paris and whom they would sometimes visit, I felt a nebulous and indescribable discomfort in the face of their ways of speaking and being, so different from those that characterized the circles in which I was now moving; or when faced with the subjects that preoccupied them, so different from my own preoccupations; or when faced with the deep, obsessive racism that flowed freely, no matter what we were talking about, and left me without any way of understanding why or how any and every subject of conversation brought us back to that. These meetings became more and more of a burden the more I went on changing into someone new. When I read the books that Annie Ernaux devotes to her parents and to the "class divide" that separates her from them, I recognized in them precisely what I was going through at this time. She provides an amazing description of the uneasiness or distress a person feels upon *returning* to her or his parents' house after not only moving out, but also after leaving behind both the family and the world to which she or he nonetheless continues to belong—the disconcerting experience of being both at home and in a foreign country.[10]

To be perfectly honest, in my case this kind of return became nearly impossible after a very few years.

Two different paths, then. Each imbricated in the other. Two interdependent trajectories for my reinvention of myself, one having to do with the sexual order, the other with the social order. And yet, when it came to writing, it was the first that I decided to analyze, the one having to do with sexual oppression, not the second which had to do with class domination. Perhaps in the theoretical gesture made by my writing I only increased the existential betrayal I was committing. For it was only one kind of personal implication of the writing subject in what is written that I took on, not the other. Indeed, one ended up excluding the other. My choice was not only a way of defining myself, of constructing my subjectivity in the present moment, it was also a choice about my past, a choice regarding the child and the teenager I had been: a gay child, a gay teenager, and not the son of a worker. And yet ...

3

"WHO'S THAT?" I asked my mother. "But that's your father!" she replied. "Don't you recognize him? It's because you hadn't seen him in such a long time." She was exactly right. I hadn't even recognized my father in a photo taken shortly before he died. Much thinner, hunched over, his gaze unfocussed, he had aged tremendously, and it took me a few minutes to make the connection between the image of this enfeebled body and the man I had known, the man who shouted at the slightest provocation, stupid and violent, the man who had inspired so much contempt in me. Suddenly I felt at sea, being confronted with the understanding that in the months, or perhaps even the years, that preceded his death, he had ceased being the person I had hated, and had instead become this pathetic figure, once a domestic tyrant, but now in decline, harmless and weak, beaten down by age and illness.

When I reread James Baldwin's beautiful text on the death of his father, one remark in particular struck me. Baldwin recounts that he put off a visit to the man he knew was very ill as long as he possibly could. Then he notes: "I had told my mother I did not want to see him because I hated him. But this was not true. It was only that I *had* hated him and I wanted to hold on to this hatred. I did not want to look on him as a ruin: it was not a ruin I had hated."

Even more striking to me was the explanation he offers: "I imagine that one of the reasons people cling to their hates so stubbornly is because they sense, once hate is gone, that they will be forced to deal with pain."[11]

Pain, or rather, in my case—since the extinguishing of the hatred I had felt did not give rise to any pain in me—an urgent obligation to figure something out about myself, a pressing desire to track backwards in time in order to understand the reasons why it had been so difficult for me to engage in even the smallest of exchanges with this man, a man who, when it comes right down to it, I had barely even known. When I really think about it, I have to admit to myself that I know next to nothing about my father. What did he think about? Or about the world he lived in? About himself? About other people? How did he see things? The circumstance of his own life? In particular, how did he see our own relationship as it became more and more difficult, more and more distant, and finally non-existent? I had a moment of stupefaction not too long ago when I learned that when he saw me on television one day, he broke down into tears, overcome by emotion. He was overwhelmed by the realization that one of his sons had achieved what seemed to him a nearly unimaginable degree of social success. And he was ready the next day, this man who had always been so homophobic, to brave the looks of his neighbors and anyone else in his village; he was even ready, should it be necessary, to defend what seemed to him to be his honor and the honor of his family. I had been speaking on television that night about my book, *Insult and the Making of the*

Gay Self, and, concerned that such an appearance might provoke sarcastic remarks and comments, he declared to my mother: "If there's any smartass who says anything to me about it, I'll smash his face in."

I never had a conversation with him, never! He wasn't capable of it (at least with me, and me with him). It's too late to spend time lamenting this. But there are plenty of questions I would now like to ask him, if only because it would help me write this book. Here again, I could only be astonished to discover these sentences in Baldwin's account: "When he was dead I realized that I had hardly ever spoken to him. When he had been dead a long time I began to wish I had." Then, describing his father's past—his father had belonged to the first generation of free black men, his father's mother having been born in the time of slavery—, he adds: "He claimed to be proud of his blackness but it had also been the cause of much humiliation and it had fixed bleak boundaries to his life."[12] Under such circumstances, it seems nearly impossible for Baldwin not to have reproached himself now and then for having abandoned his family, for having betrayed his own kind. His mother never understood why he left, why he went to live so far away, first to Greenwich Village so he could be a part of the literary circles there, and then to France. Would it have been possible for him to stay? Obviously not. He had to leave, to leave Harlem behind, to leave behind his father's narrow-mindedness, his sanctimonious hostility towards culture and literature, the suffocating atmosphere of the family home. How else could he become a writer, how else live openly his homosexuality (and take up in his work the double question of what it means to be black and to be gay)? Yet still the moment came where the necessity of a "going back" made itself felt, even if it was after the death of his father (in reality his stepfather, but still, the person who raised him from the earliest years of his childhood). The text that he writes to pay homage to this man might therefore be interpreted as his means of accomplishing, or at least of beginning, this mental "return," the effort to understand who this person actually was, a man he had so detested and so wanted to get away from. Perhaps too, beginning this process of historical and political deliberation would allow him one day to reclaim his own past on an emotional level, to get to a place where he could not only understand, but also accept himself. It's easy enough to see why, obsessed as he was by this question, he would insist so strongly in an interview that "to avoid the journey back is to avoid the Self, to avoid 'life'."[13]

As had been the case for Baldwin with his father, so I began to realize that everything my father had been, which is to say everything I held against him, all the reasons I had detested him, had been shaped by the violence of the social world. My father had been proud to belong to the working class. Later on, he was proud to have risen, however modestly, above that condition. Yet his condition had been the cause of any number of humiliations and had set "bleak boundaries" to his life. It had planted a kind of madness in him that he never overcame and that made him nearly incapable of sustaining relationships with other people.

Like Baldwin in his quite different context, I am certain that my father bore within him the weight of a crushing history that could not help but produce serious psychic damage in those who lived through it. My father's life, his personality, his subjectivity had been doubly marked and determined by a place and by a time whose particular hardships and constraints continually played off each other in a way that only made them proliferate. Here is the key to his being: where and when he was born, the timespan and the region of social space in which it was decided what his place in the world would be, his apprenticeship of the world, his relationship to the world. The near-madness of my father and the impaired relational abilities that resulted from it had, in the final analysis, nothing psychological about them, if by psychological we mean a link to some kind of individual character trait. They were the effect of the precisely situated being-in-the-world that was his.

Just like Baldwin's mother, my mother said to me: "He worked long hours so you'd have enough to eat." Then she went on to speak to me about him, leaving aside her own grievances: "Don't judge him too harshly. His life wasn't an easy one." He was born in 1929, the oldest child in what was to become a large family. His mother had twelve children. It can be hard today to imagine how many women were destined to become slaves to mother-hood. Twelve children! Two of them were stillborn (or else died very young). Another, who was born on the open road during the evacuation of the city in 1940, while German planes were ruthlessly attacking the columns of refugees, was mentally disabled, perhaps because it hadn't been possible to cut the umbilical cord normally, or perhaps because he was injured when my grandmother threw herself and him into the ditch to protect him from the machine gun fire, or perhaps simply because he didn't receive the kind of care that is required imme-diately after birth. Who knows which of these different stories retained in the family memory is the right one. My grandmother kept him with her throughout her life. I always heard that it was for the sake of the social security subsidy, because that subsidy was crucial to the economic survival of the family. When I was young, my brother and I were terrified of him. He drooled, only expressed himself in strange rumblings, and would stretch out his arms towards us, perhaps seeking a bit of affection, or perhaps offering some. Yet he never received any in response; we would shrink away, when we weren't screaming or actively pushing him away. In retrospect, I am mortified by our behavior, and yet we were only children at the time, and he was a grown-up whom others called "abnormal."

As I mentioned, my father's family had been obliged to leave the city during the war, taking part in what was called the "exodus." They ended up far from home, on a farm near Mimizan, a small town in the Landes. Having spent several months there, they came back to Reims as soon as the armistice was signed. The north of France was occupied by the German army. (I was born long after the end of the war, and still the only word used in my family to talk about Germans was "les Boches," for whom there was a fierce and seemingly inextinguishable hatred. It wasn't at all uncommon, well into the 1970s and beyond, to end a meal by proclaiming: "One more that the *Boches* won't get their hands on!"[14] I have to confess that I have myself used the expression more than once.)

In 1940, my father was 11 years old, and every day until he was 14 or 15, during the entire period of the Occupation, he would have to go out to neighboring villages to find food for his family—in wind, rain or snow, no matter what the weather. He would sometimes have to cover as much as 20 kilometers on his bicycle in the freezing cold typical of the Champagne region's severe winter, to find potatoes or some other foodstuff. He was in charge of nearly everything at home.

They had moved into a fairly large house—I'm not sure if this was during the war or just after—in the middle of a housing complex built in the 1920s for large working class families. It was the kind of house that had been thought up by a group of Catholic industrialists who, at the outset of the twentieth century, set out to improve the housing conditions of their workers. Reims was a city divided in two by a conspicuous class barrier. On one side of the divide was the upper middle class, and on the other the impoverished workers. The philanthropic societies of the former worried about the poor living conditions of the latter, and about the harmful consequences arising from them. Worries about a declining birthrate had produced a remarkable change in attitudes towards large families: if, up until the end of the nineteenth century, they had been considered by reformers and demographers to be one of the causes of disorder and of juvenile delinquency, at the beginning of the twentieth century, they became an essential bastion of defense against the depopulation that was threatening to weaken a nation confronted by foreign enemies. If these large families had once been stigmatized and combatted by the supporters of Mathusianism, now the dominant discourse—on both the left and the right—was bent on encouraging them, valorizing them, and therefore also supporting them. Propaganda in support of a rising birthrate now went hand in hand with urban renewal projects so that these new pillars of the revived nation could have decent living spaces. It was hoped that such spaces would make it possible to ward off dangers that had often been emphasized by bourgeois reformers, dangers associated with a working class childhood in which poor living conditions meant that children spent too much time on the streets: an anarchic proliferation of rough boys and immoral girls.[15]

Inspired by these new political and patriotic points of view, philanthropists from the Champagne region founded an organization whose function was to build affordable housing. It was called the *"Foyer rémois"* [Habitations of Reims], and its charge was to construct housing projects offering living quarters that were spacious, clean, and healthy, intended for families with more than four children, with three bedrooms—one for the parents, one for the boys, and one for the girls. They didn't have a bathroom, but they did have running water. (The inhabitants washed themselves one at a time at the kitchen sink.) A concern with physical cleanliness was, of course, only one aspect of these city planning programs. Moral hygiene was another primary consideration. The idea was, by encouraging a high birthrate and family values, to wean workers away from bars and the alcoholism they facilitated. Political concerns were also not absent. The bourgeoisie imagined it might in this way put a check on socialist and union propaganda that it worried might flourish in working class meeting places outside the home, just as, in the 1930s, it hoped by the same means to shield the workers from communist influences. Domestic happiness, at least the way the bourgeois philanthropists imagined it for poor people, was meant to keep these workers invested in their home life and to divert them from the temptations of political resistance and its forms of organization and action. In 1914 the war interrupted the implementation of all these programs. After the four apocalyptic years that swept over northeast France, especially the region around Reims, everything had to be rebuilt. (Photographs taken in 1918 of what was called at the time the "martyred city" are terrifying: as far as the eye can see, there are only fragments of walls left standing amidst piles of rubble. It is as if some malicious god had gone out of his way to wipe this area off the map, an area saturated with history, sparing only the Cathedral and the Saint-Remi Basilica. And even they were severely damaged by the deluge of fire and iron that rained down on them.) Thanks to American aid, city planners and architects built up a new city from the ruins, and around the perimeter of that city they laid out the famous "garden cities," housing tracts in the "regionalist style" (although, if I'm not mistaken, the style was in fact Alsatian). Some of the houses were single family dwellings, some were duplexes or town houses. All of them had a yard, and all were built along wide streets with interspersed green spaces.[16]

My grandparents moved into one of these housing projects either during or shortly after World War II. When I was a child, towards the end of the 1950s and the early 1960s, the spaces dreamed up and then realized by the philanthropists had deteriorated quite a bit. The Foyer rémois "garden city" in which my grandparents and their youngest children still lived had been poorly maintained, and was utterly rundown, eaten away at by the very poverty it had been devoted to housing, a poverty that was everywhere visible. It was an extremely unhealthy environment, and in fact incubated many different social pathologies. In purely statistical terms, a drift into delinquency was one of the prime options open to young people from the neighborhood. This of course remains the case today in those similarly appointed spaces of urban and social segregation—the historical durability of these phenomena is striking. One of my father's brothers became a thief, went to prison, and was banned from Reims; we would catch glimpses of him from time to time, sneaking in at nightfall to see his parents or to ask his brothers and sisters for money. He had long been absent from my life and from my memory when I learned from my mother that he had become a street person, and had in fact died in the street. As a young man he had been a sailor. (He did his required military service in the navy, and had then enlisted permanently before being discharged because of his conduct—fights, thefts, and the like.) It was his face, in profile, from a photograph of him in uniform that my grandparents had on the buffet in their dining room, that came to my mind when I first read *Querelle*. In general, petty or serious crimes were the rule in the neighborhood, as if they constituted some kind of obstinate popular resistance to the laws imposed by a state that was perceived on a daily basis to be an instrument wielded by a class enemy, an enemy whose power was visible any and everywhere, all the time.

In accordance with the initial desires of the Catholic bourgeoisie and with what it considered to be the "moral values" it wished to inculcate in the popular classes, the birth rate was a healthy one. It wasn't unusual for families in the houses close to that of my grandparents to have 14 or 15 children, or even 21, my mother claims, even though I have a hard time believing this could have been possible. Yet the Communist Party also thrived. Actual membership was reasonably common, at least among the men. As for the women, while sharing their husbands' opinions, they nonetheless stayed away from organized political activities and "cell meetings." But official membership wasn't even necessary for a certain feeling of political belonging to spread and perpetuate itself. The feeling was spontaneously and tightly tied up with the social situation of the people involved. People spoke easily about the "Party." My grandfather, my father and his brothers—and also on my mother's side, her step father and her half-brother—commonly went as a group to attend the public meetings organized by national party leaders at regular intervals. Everyone voted for the Communist candidate at every election, ranting about the false left that the socialists represented—their compromises, their betrayals. But then, in the runoff, they would grudgingly cast their vote for the socialist when they had to, in the name of realism or the "republican discipline" no one dared go against. (Yet in these years, Communist candidates were often in the strongest position, so this kind of situation only rarely presented itself.) The words "the Left" really meant something important. People wanted to defend their own interests, to make their voices heard, and the way to achieve that—aside from strikes or protests—was to delegate, to hand oneself over to the "representatives of the working class" and to political leaders whose decisions were thus implicitly accepted and whose discourses you learned and repeated. You became a political subject by putting yourself into the hands of the party spokespersons, through whom the workers, the "working class," came to exist as an organized group, as a class that was aware of itself as such. One's way of thinking about oneself, the values one espoused, the attitudes one adopted were all to a large extent shaped by the conception of the world that the "Party" helped to inculcate in people's minds and to diffuse throughout the social body. To vote was to participate in an important moment of collective self-affirmation, a moment that affirmed your political significance as well. So on election nights, when the results came in, people would explode with anger upon learning that the right had won yet again and would rail against the "scabs" who had voted for the Gaullists, and thereby voted against themselves.

How easy it has become to deplore the communist influence over various (but not all) populist milieus from the 1950s through the 1970s. It is worth remembering the meaning that influence had for all those people whom it is now all the more easy to criticize since it is so unlikely they could make themselves heard in a public forum. (Are they ever offered a chance to speak? What means of their own do they have to do so?) To be communist had next to nothing to do with a desire to establish a government resembling the one found in the U.S.S.R. "Foreign" policy, in any case, seemed a distant concern, as is often the case amid the popular classes—and even more so for women than for men. It was a given that one took the Soviet side against American imperialism, but the topic almost never came up. And even though the military enforcement operations that the Red Army carried out against friendly nations were disconcerting, we preferred not to talk about them: In 1968, as the radio covered the tragic events unfolding in Prague after the Soviet intervention, I asked my parents "What is going on?" and found myself sharply rebuked by my mother: "What do you care? It's none of your business." Surely this was because in fact she had no answer to give me, and was as perplexed as was I, a mere 15 year old. In fact, the reasons people adhered to communist values were linked to more immediate and more concrete preoccupations. When in his *Abécédaire*, Gilles Deleuze puts forward the idea that "being on the left" means "first of all being aware of the world," "being aware of what's on the horizon" (by which he means considering that the most urgent problems are those of the third world, which are closer to us than the problems of our own neighborhood), whereas "not being on the left" would, in contrary fashion, mean being focused on the street where one lives, on the country one inhabits, the definition he offers is diametrically opposed to the one incarnated by my parents.[17] In working class environments, a leftist politics meant first and foremost a very pragmatic rejection of the experience of one's own daily life. It was a form of protest, and not a political project inspired by a global perspective. You considered what was right around you, not what was far off, either in time or in space. Even if people were always saying things like, "what we need is a good revolution," these pat expressions were linked to the hardships of daily life and to the intolerable nature of the injustices around them rather than to any perspective involving the establishment of a different political system. Given that everything that happened seemed to have been decided by some hidden power ("that was no accident"), invoking the "revolution"—without any idea of where or when or how it might break out—seemed one's only recourse (it was one myth against another) in the fight against the powers of evil—the Right, the rich, the bigwigs—who inflicted so much hardship on the lives of the poor, of "people like us."

My family divided the world into two camps, those who were "for the workers" and those who were "against the workers," or, in slightly different words, those who "defended the workers" and those who "did nothing for the workers." How many times did I hear sentences that encapsulated this political attitude and the choices that resulted from it! On one side there was "us" and those who were "with us"; on the other side was "them."[18]

Nowadays who fulfills the role played by the "Party"? To whom can exploited and powerless people turn in order to feel that they are supported or that their point of view is expressed? To whom can they refer, who can they lean on, in order to provide themselves with a political existence and a cultural identity? Or in order to feel proud of themselves because they have been legitimized and because this legitimation has come from a powerful source? A source that, in the simplest terms, takes into account who they are, how they live, what they think about, what they want?

When my father watched the news, the remarks he made revealed a visceral allergic reaction to both the right and the extreme right. During the presidential campaign of 1965 and then during and after May 1968 he would lose his temper simply upon hearing the voice of Tixier-Vignancour, a figure who seemed a caricature of the old French extreme right. When Tixier-Vignancour denounced "the red flag of Communism" that people were waving in the streets of Paris, my father fulminated: "the red flag is the flag of the workers!" A bit later he would feel himself attacked and offended by the way Giscard d'Estaing, through the medium of the television, would manage to inflict on all French households his grand bourgeois manner, his affected gestures, his grotesque manner of speaking. My father would also direct his insults at the journalists who hosted political programs, and would be overjoyed when someone he considered a spokesperson for his own thoughts and feelings (this or that Stalinist apparatchik with a worker's accent) would manage to break the rules of the television program in a way no one would dare do today, given how nearly total the obedience of most political figures and intellectuals has become to the powers of the media. To break the rules meant to speak about the real problems affecting workers instead of responding to the typically political questions to which the discussion was supposed to be limited. To break the rules meant to do justice to all those whose voices are never heard under these kinds of circumstances, to those whose very existence is systematically excluded from the landscape of legitimate politics.

4

I REMEMBER THE YARD behind my grandparents' house. It wasn't very big, and was separated by a fence on both sides from the identical yards of their neighbors. At the far end, there was a hut (and this was the case for most of the houses in the neighborhood) where my grandmother raised rabbits. We would feed them grass and carrots until finally they would end up on our plates on a Sunday or a holiday. My grandmother could neither read nor write. She would ask people to read to her or to write official letters for her, and would offer vague apologies for her deficiency: "I don't know my letters," she would say, in a tone that suggested neither anger nor rebelliousness, but rather a submission to reality, a kind of resignation that characterized all of her gestures and all of the words she spoke and that perhaps enabled her to endure her situation, to accept it as an inevitability. My grandfather was a cabinetmaker; he worked in a furniture factory. To make ends meet, he would build furniture at home for the neighbors. He received lots of orders from near and far, in fact, and literally worked himself to death in order to feed his family, never taking a day off. I was still a child when he died at the age of 54 of throat cancer. (That was a plague that carried off many workers in those years, as all of them smoked an unimaginable number of cigarettes each day. Three of my father's brothers would die quite young from the same cause, another having died even younger from alcoholism.) When I was a teenager, my grandmother was astonished by the fact that I didn't smoke. "It's healthier if a man smokes," she would say to me, totally unaware of all the damage such a belief continued to inflict all around her. Of frail health herself, she would die ten or so years after her husband, doubtless from exhaustion: she was 62 years old when she died and was cleaning offices to earn her living. One winter's night, after work, she slipped on a patch of ice on her way home to the miniscule two room apartment in a low income housing complex where she had ended up. She hit her head hard when she fell, and never recovered, dying a few days after the accident.

There is really no doubt that this "garden city" where my father lived before I was born, and that was one of the major scenes of my childhood (my brother and I spent a lot of time there, especially during vacations), was a place of social ostracism. It was a reservation for the poor, set off from the center of town and from the well-to-do neighborhoods. And yet, when I think back on it, I realize that it didn't resemble what we nowadays refer to with the word "projects." It was a horizontal living environment, not a vertical one: no apartment buildings, no towers, nothing of the architecture that would appear at the end of the 1950s and in a major way throughout the 1960s and 1970s. There thus remained something of a human character about this area on the fringes of the city. Even if the area had a bad reputation, even if it resembled a destitute ghetto, it wasn't all that unpleasant to live in. Working class traditions, notably certain kinds of culture and solidarity, had managed to develop and perpetuate themselves. It was thanks to one of these forms of culture, the Saturday night dance, that my parents met. My mother lived not far off, in a suburb closer to the city, with her mother and her mother's partner. Both my mother and my father, like all of the working class youth at the time, enjoyed the diversion and the moment of happiness provided by popular neighborhood dances. Such dances have for the most part disappeared today, pretty much only still occurring on July 14 or the night before. Yet at the time in question they were for many the only "outing" of the week, an occasion for friends to meet up and for amorous and sexual encounters. Couples formed and dissolved. Sometimes they lasted. My mother had a crush on another fellow, but he wanted to sleep with her, and she didn't. She was afraid of getting pregnant and having a baby with no father should the fellow prefer to break up rather than accepting an unsought role as father. She had no desire to have a baby who would be obliged to live through what she had had to live through, and what had caused her so much suffering. The fellow her heart had chosen left her for someone else. She met my father. She never loved him, but she told herself, "it'll be him or someone just like him." She wanted some independence, and marriage was the only way to obtain it, since one only became a legal adult at age 21. In any case, they had to wait until my father reached that age. My paternal grandmother didn't want him to leave home, since she wanted him to "chip in his pay" as long as she could make him. As soon as it was possible, he married my mother. She was 20 years old.

At the time, my father had already been working—at the lowest rung on the ladder—for quite a while. He hadn't even reached the age of fourteen (school ended in June, and he began working right away, and only turned fourteen three months later) when he found himself in the surroundings that would be his for the rest of his life, chasing the only horizon that was open to him: the factory. It was waiting for him; he was waiting for it. It was also waiting for his brothers and sisters, who would all follow in his footsteps. And it waited, and still waits, for those who were born and are born into families with the same social identity as his. Social determinism had a grip on him from the day he was born. There was no escape for him from that to which he had been promised by all the laws, all the mechanisms, of what there is no other word for than "reproduction."

My father's education thus went no further than middle school. No one would have imagined it could have been otherwise, neither his parents nor himself. In his world, you went to school until the age of fourteen, because that was required, and you left school at age 14, because it was no longer required. That's the way things were. To drop out of school was certainly no scandal. Quite the contrary. I remember how indignant everyone in my family was when school was made mandatory until age 16. "What's the point in making kids stay in school if they don't want to, if they'd rather be working?" was what people repeated, never stopping to wonder about how a like or a dislike for school might be distributed differentially across society. Selection within the educational system often happens by a process of self-elimination, and that self-elimination is treated as if it were freely chosen: extended studies are for other kinds of people, for "people of means," and it just happens that those people turn out to be the ones who like going to school. The field of possibilities—and even the field of possibilities that it is possible to imagine, to say nothing of the field of possibilities that can actually be realized—is tightly circumscribed by one's class position. It was as if the barrier between social worlds was utterly impermeable. The boundaries that divide these worlds help define within each of them radically different ways of perceiving what it is possible to be or to become, of perceiving what it is possible to aspire to or not. People know that things are different elsewhere, but that elsewhere seems part of a far off and inaccessible universe. So much so that people feel neither excluded from nor deprived of all sorts of things because they have no access to what, in those far off social realms, constitutes a self-evident norm. It's in the order of things, and there's nothing more to be said about it. No one thinks about how the order of things actually works, because to do so would require being able to see oneself from a different point of view, have a bird's eye view on one's own life and the lives of other people. Only if you actually manage to move from one side of the border to the other, as happened in my case, can you get out from under the implacable logic of all those things that go without saying in order to perceive the terrible injustice of this unequal distribution of prospects and possibilities. And things haven't changed all that much: the age for leaving school has shifted, but the social barrier between classes remains the same. That is why any sociology or any philosophy that begins by placing at the center of its project the "point of view of the actors" and the "meaning they give to their actions" runs the risk of simply reproducing a shorthand version of the mystified relation that social agents maintain with their own practices and desires, and consequently does nothing more than serve to perpetuate the world as it currently stands—an ideology of justification (for the established order). Only an epistemological break with the way in which individuals spontaneously think about themselves renders possible the description of the mechanisms by which the social order reproduces itself. The entire system needs to be apprehended, including the manner in which dominated people ratify their domination through the choice they make to drop out of school, thereby making the choice they had been intended to make. A theory's power and interest lie precisely in the fact that it doesn't consider it as sufficient simply to record the words that "actors" say about their "actions," but that rather, it sets as a goal to allow both individuals and groups to see and to think differently about what they are and what they do, and then, perhaps, to change what they do and what they are. It is a matter of breaking with incorporated categories of perception and established frameworks of meaning, and thereby with the social inertia of which these categories and frameworks are the vectors; after such a break, the goal is to produce a new way of looking at the world and thereby to open up new political perspectives.

For social destinies are sketched out incredibly early! Things have been arranged ahead of time. Verdicts have been handed down before it's even possible to be aware of it. Our sentences are burned into the skin of our shoulder with a red hot iron at the moment of our birth, and the places allocated to us have been defined and delimited by what has come before us: the past of the family and the surroundings into which we are born. My father wasn't even given the chance to earn a general education certificate, the one that represented, for working-class children, the crowning achievement of their education. Children of the bourgeoisie were on a different track. At the age of eleven, they started high school, whereas working class children and children from farming families were restricted to elementary and middle schools until age fourteen, when their education ended. There was to be no confusion between those to whom one was to mete out the rudiments of the practical education (reading, writing, and arithmetic) that was needed to cope with daily life and sufficient for carrying out manual labor, and those, coming from more privileged classes, who had a right to become "cultured," to be given access to a culture that was "disinterested," access to "culture" pure and simple. And of course it was feared that such culture could only exercise a corrupting influence on workers were they to be exposed to it.[19] The certificate in question involved the acquisition of basic functional forms of knowledge (with a few other elements thrown in from the "history of France"—a few dates of the main events in the national mythology, and from "Geography"—a list of the different administrative divisions of France and their capital cities). It was an important credential for those for whom it was intended, and in those circles it was a point of pride to have obtained it. Only half of those who took the required exam actually passed it. And there were many people, such as my father, who, having more or less abandoned school even before the legal age for doing so, didn't make it that far. Most of what my father learned, he learned on his own, later, by taking night classes after finishing work for the day. His hope was to be able to climb up several rungs on the social ladder. For a while he dreamed of becoming an industrial draftsman. He soon woke up to a cold reality. Perhaps he didn't have the necessary educational background. Above all, it must have been difficult to concentrate after working a full day at the factory. He was forced to abandon his studies along with his illusions. For a long time he saved a few large sheets of squared paper, covered in charts and sketches—course assignments?—that he would sometimes take out of their folder and look over, or show to us, before returning them to the bottom of the drawer where he kept his broken dreams. Not only did he remain a worker, but he had to be one twice over: when I was very young he began his day very early in the morning and worked in a factory until the early afternoon. Then at the end of the afternoon he went to a different factory to work a few more hours to add to his salary. My mother helped as much as she could, wearing herself out cleaning houses and doing laundry. (Washing machines didn't yet exist, or were extremely rare, and doing other people's laundry was a way of earning a bit of money to add to the household income.) It was only when my father was caught in a long period of unemployment in 1970 that my mother herself would go to work in a factory, but she kept on working there even after my father found work again. (I now understand that she took on factory work so that I could finish high school—take the baccalaureate exam—and go to college. It was something I never thought of at the time, or else I repressed it as deeply as I could, even in the face of my mother bringing up the possibility that I might do the responsible thing and start earning my keep and helping the family—a possibility, if truth be told, that she mentioned quite frequently.) My father kept trotting out the notion that "a factory is no place for a woman," but to no avail. Whatever the damage done to his masculine sense of honor by not being able to provide for his household on his own, he had no choice but to resign himself to the fact that my mother became a "worker," taking on all the pejorative connotations that attached to the idea of a woman who worked in a factory: loose women whose speech was crude, who maybe slept around—in short, tarts. This bourgeois image of the working class woman who worked outside the home and alongside men was also widely shared by working class men who didn't like to give up control over their spouses or partners for several hours each day, and who were terrified by the abhorrent image of the liberated woman. Annie Ernaux writes of her mother, who took up employment in a factory when she was quite young, that she insisted on being considered one of the "factory girls, *but nonetheless* respectable." Yet the simple fact that she worked alongside men "meant that she would never be seen as a 'decent young girl,' which was what she had always longed to be."[20] The situation was the same for older women: the kind of work they did sufficed to give them all a bad reputation, whether or not they took advantage of the sexual freedom imputed to them. The result was that my father would frequently go sit in a café near the factory at the time my mother got off work so that he would know if my mother secretly stopped in upon leaving work, and be able to catch her by surprise if she did. But she didn't—neither that café nor any other. She headed home to make dinner after having done the shopping. Like all working women, she had a second job waiting for her at home.

It would only be much later that my father would manage to rise up a few rungs in the social hierarchy, at least in the hierarchy at the factory, moving up from the category of an unskilled worker to that of a skilled worker, and finally to that of supervisor. He was no longer a worker, but rather supervised them. Or, more precisely, he was the head of a team. He took a very simple kind of pride in this new status, which provided him with an improved sense of self-worth. Of course, I found all of this laughable at the time, but then I was the person who, many years later, would still blush with shame when, applying for this or that official document, I would be obliged to provide a copy of my birth certificate listing the first professions of my father (unskilled worker) and my mother (cleaning lady)—the same person who hadn't been able to understand why my parents had been so eager to improve their situation, even in a way that while miniscule to my eyes, was obviously extremely significant to theirs.

As I was saying, my father worked in a factory from the age of 14 to that of 56, when he was given "early retirement," whether he wanted it or not, and in the same year as my mother (at age 55), both of them spit out by the system that had exploited them so shamelessly. He found himself at loose ends with too much time on his hands, whereas she was happy to leave a workplace where the work was so exhausting—to a degree unimaginable to anyone who hasn't experienced it—and where the noise, the heat, and the daily repetition of the same mechanical movements slowly wore away at the health of even the most resilient organisms. They were tired, worn out. My mother hadn't contributed to social security for long enough (her work cleaning houses had always been off the books), which meant that her retirement payments were correspondingly lower, and so their income dropped notably when they retired. They rearranged their life as best they could. For example, they traveled more often—a weekend in London, a week in Spain or Turkey—thanks to the workers' organization of the factory where my father had worked. It's not that they loved each other any more than they had in the past. They had simply found a *modus vivendi*; they were used to each other; and they both knew that only the death of one or the other of them would separate them.

My father was handy at many things, and proud to be so, just as he was proud of manual labor in general. It was in these kinds of activities that he flourished, and he spent all his free time on them. He knew what fine work was, and he appreciated it. When I was in one of the last two years of high school, he turned an old table into a desk for me. He installed cabinets, and fixed whatever needed fixing in the apartment. I, on the other hand, was all thumbs. Perhaps willfully so (for after all couldn't I have chosen to learn something from him?) given how invested I was in not resembling him, in becoming something socially different from what he was. Later I would discover that certain intellectual types could also be quite handy, and that it was in fact possible to be bookish—to read books and to write them—while still enjoying practical tasks and manual kinds of work. Discovering this would leave me utterly perplexed. It was as if my whole personality was called into question by the destabilization of what I had perceived and experienced as a fundamental, a defining opposition (but obviously only defining in my particular case). With sports it was the same thing. Learning that many of my friends watched sports on television was deeply disturbing to me, causing a principle whose solidity had imposed itself powerfully upon me to dissolve before my eyes. For me, in order to define myself as an intellectual, as part of my very desire to be an intellectual, I had felt required to experience as intolerable nights spent watching soccer matches on television. The culture of sports, sports as one's only interest (for men, since for women it was mostly popular news items), these were aspects of reality that I had been intent on deprecating, on disdaining out of a sense of superiority. It took me quite a while to break down all these dividing walls that had been necessary for me to become who I had become, to reintegrate into my mental and existential universe all these dimensions that I had shut out.

When I was a child, my parents got around on a moped. They carried us, my brother and I, on kids' seats attached behind them. That arrangement could prove to be dangerous. One day, while my father was negotiating a curve, the bike slipped on some gravel and my brother's leg was broken. In 1963, they got their driver's licenses and bought a used car. (I can be seen at the age of 12 or 13 leaning against the hood of that black Simca Aronde in a number of photographs my mother gave me.) My mother passed the driver's exam before my father. For my father, the idea of sitting in the passenger seat and being driven around by his wife was so degrading that he preferred driving without a license for a while in order to avoid any such ignominious situation. He would literally go crazy, and turn quite nasty, when my mother would voice her concern and express her intention to take what he considered to be his place. Then, after a while, things sorted themselves out: it would always be he who drove. (Even when he had had too much to drink he wouldn't let her drive.) On Sundays, once we had a car, we would go on picnics to forests or fields outside the town. It was never a question of taking a summer vacation. We didn't have the money. Our trips only extended as far as a day's visit to a nearby town: Nancy, Laon, or Charleville, for example. We even crossed the border into Belgium to visit a town called Bouillon. (We learned to associate this name with Godefroy de Bouillon and his adventures in the Crusades; but since then I have come more willingly to associate it with Cilea's opera, *Adriana Lecouvreur*, and with the terrible and imposing character from that opera, the Princess de Bouillon.) We toured the chateau and bought chocolate and souvenirs, but went no farther. It wasn't until much later that I would get to know Brussels. Once we even went to Verdun, and I remember a gloomy and frightening visit to the Douaumont Ossuary, where the remains of the soldiers who died in battle there during the first World War are gathered. That visit gave me nightmares for a long time. We also sometimes went to Paris to visit my maternal grandmother. Parisian traffic jams would send my father into astounding fits of rage. He would stamp his feet, utter streams of obscenities and cries of anger, without anyone really understanding why he was working himself up into such a state. The result of this would be endless arguments with my mother, who had little patience for what she referred to as his "*cinéma*," his crazy song and dance. The same things happened every time he drove. If he took the wrong road, or missed a turn, he would start screaming as if the world were about to end. But most frequently of all, when the weather was good, we would drive along the banks of the Marne, in champagne country, and spend hours engaged in my father's favorite relaxing pastime: fishing. At these moments it was as if he became a different man, and there was a bond that passed between him and his children: he taught us all the gestures and techniques we needed, he gave us advice, and we would spend the day commenting on what happened or what didn't. "They're really biting today," or "Not even a nibble." And we would speculate as to why, blaming the heat or the rain, the earliness or lateness of the season, and so on. Sometimes we would meet up with my aunts and uncles and their children. In the evening we'd eat the fish we had caught. My mother would clean them, dip them in flour, and fry them up. It was a royal feast for us. But with the passage of time, I came to find all this pointless and silly. I wanted to spend my time reading, not to waste it with a fishing rod in hand watching a piece of cork bob up and down on the surface of the water. Soon I hated all the cultural aspects of this activity, all the forms of sociability associated with it: the music playing from the transistor radios, the meaningless chit chat with the people you'd meet, the strict division of labor between men (who fished) and the women (who knitted and read photo romances, or took care of the kids and the cooking). I stopped going with my parents on these outings. To invent myself, I had first of all to disassociate myself from all of that.

1

WHEN MY MOTHER WAS BORN, her mother was only 17 years old. It's unlikely that the young man with whom my grandmother had committed her "transgression" was any older. Her father kicked her out when he realized she was pregnant. "You and your bastard can get lost. To hell with the both of you!" he yelled at her. So she left. Soon thereafter she opened her own door to her own mother. (I'm not sure why, but I imagine it's because her mother wasn't willing to give up seeing her daughter, so instead she left her husband.) The lover of this very young woman didn't put up with the new situation for long. Their apartment must have been tiny. So he told her, "It's either me or your mother. You choose." She chose her mother. He left and she never heard from him again. He was thus only involved in raising his child for a couple months, after which he disappeared from my mother's life, my mother the "*bâtarde,*" at a time when she was still too young to have any memories of him. Soon after, my grandmother met and set up house with another man with whom she would have three other children. My mother lived with them until the war broke out. The war would change her life forever. In later years she would beg her mother to tell her the name of the man she had never known, asking if she knew what had happened to him. The only response she ever received was,

"It's no use stirring up the past." All that she knows about her father is that he was very good looking and that he was a construction worker—and that he was Spanish. "Andalusian," she claimed to me recently. She likes to think that he was a gypsy, as if writing herself into a family romance of that kind could help make bearable all the pain that figures among the devastating consequences of being a girl with no father. (She can still easily recall the wound—one that still smarts—inflicted on her by a schoolteacher when, as a very young child, she had responded in class to a routine question about her parents by saying she didn't have a father: "Everyone has a father," the woman objected with a snicker. But in point of fact she didn't have one.) And really, it's not at all impossible that this gypsy fable could be true. Seeing photos of myself at the age of 15 or 16 with my dark complexion and long, curly, black hair, it has occurred to me that I might have inherited some of these genetic traits from such a relative. A few years ago, while on one of those trips organized by the worker's organization at my father's factory, my mother and father were touring Andalusia. As the bus approached Grenada, my mother felt a shiver of emotion. As she told me later, "It was bizarre, the way I shivered. I have no idea what was happening, but I'm sure it was because it was my country. And then one day we were having lunch in a restaurant and there were some gypsies playing the guitar. One of them came and sat next to me and said, 'You are one of us.'"

While I have never subscribed to this kind of mystical feeling about one's origins—I don't really understand what phantasm regarding biological origins or what psychology of deep family bonds it arises from—I certainly understand that my mother has always, up to and including today, had difficulty dealing with the fact that she never knew her father, and that deep inside herself she invented out of various bits of reality her own version of Spain, as a ray of sunshine that could rescue her from the northern fog and from the gloomy reality of her own life. Her dreams in life were not of becoming rich, but rather of light and of freedom. Perhaps more education would have allowed her to pursue that dream of freedom. "I would have liked to be a school teacher," she says today, because "in those days, that's a thing a woman could do after finishing school." Her ambitions were small ones, and yet even so, they proved unrealistic. Just at the moment when she would have entered high school (this was already something that was unheard of for someone from her background, but she had always been a good student and had even been authorized to skip a grade when she was 10 years old), her family had to leave town: people were encouraged to evacuate in the face of the invasion of the German army. Buses carried residents south. Only looters remained behind, or those determined to prevent looters from stealing their belongings. (Such is my mother's version of this grim episode.) This journey led them to Burgundy, where they were lodged on a farm.

During the time they spent there, my grandmother worked in the fields from dawn to dusk. The children passed the time however they could, playing in the yard or helping with house-hold tasks. Once the armistice was signed, everyone went back home. My grandmother found a job in a metal factory. Then when a call was made for volunteers to go work in Germany, she applied. She left her partner and put her four children in the care of a foster family. After a few months, she stopped sending money, and the foster family sent the two boys and the two girls to a public home for orphans and abandoned children. That put an end to any chance my mother might have had of attending high school. She did attempt and obtain her general education certificate, and was (and still is) very proud of this accomplishment. Shortly thereafter a place was found for her as a maid. For the policy at this public orphanage was to find work for children in its care as soon as they turned fourteen. For boys it would be on a farm (as happened to her older brother), and for girls it was housework.

My mother's first job was working for a couple of teachers. They were good people, and they took a liking to her. She still remembers them with gratitude, because while she worked for them, they paid for her to take courses in stenography, with the idea that she might become a secretary some day. She excelled at her lessons, and would have liked to keep going. A single year wasn't long enough to become professionally qualified. However a year was the maximum length of time the state organization would keep young girls in a single "place." After that, they had to change employers. So once more, my mother had to give up her dreams. A cleaning woman she was, and a cleaning woman she would remain.

As occupations go, it wasn't an easy one. Sexual harassment was a constant feature of this kind of work. Several times, the husband of the woman who had hired her would try to set up a discreet meeting. When she didn't show up, the result was that she would be fired the next day, after the husband told his wife that my mother had been making advances. There was even one time where the father of the woman employing her came up behind her and grabbed her breasts. She freed herself brusquely, but made no complaint since that would only have meant losing her job and having to find another: "Who would have believed me? Who would have taken the word of a silly little maid against that of one of the town's rich factory owners?" she confided to me once she had agreed to tell me the story of her past. When she spoke of this part of her past, she couldn't help falling back, sixty years later, into a state of cold, but also saddened, anger. Then she added, "these things happened all the time, but people kept their mouths shut. Back then it wasn't like today. Women had no rights.... Men made all the rules." Already at the age of 16 or 17, she understood what men were like and so, when she did marry, she did so without any illusions about men in general or about the particular man she was marrying.

On returning to France after her time in Germany, my grandmother moved back in with the man she had been with before the war, and took back the three children she had had with him. But she didn't take back her eldest; she didn't even make an effort to find out where she was or what she was doing. And yet back before the war had started, my mother, who now lived with her employers, had been living with her mother and step-father alongside her two half-brothers and her half-sister. Her fervent wish had been to think of her step-father as her father. He was a coalman, and would pass through the streets with a horse-drawn cart crying "Coalman! Coalman!" Those who wanted to buy sacks of coal would call to him from their windows. He continued in the same occupation after the war, although the horse-drawn cart had been replaced by a small van. When my grandmother married him, in 1946, she didn't bother to invite her daughter to the wedding. My mother would learn about it from her brother, with whom she had stayed in contact. A little while later, despite everything, feeling quite lonely and unhappy, she made up her mind to visit the woman who had treated her so atrociously. ("She was still my mother, and when it came right down to it I didn't have anyone else.") But my grandmother had left town. She had headed in the direction of Paris, where her sister lived, taking her other children with her. In Paris, or in the town on the outskirts of Paris where she settled, it seems she indulged in frequent amorous or sexual dalliances. "She was the kind of woman who broke up homes," is what a person said of her to my mother one day. Yet in the end she would come back to Reims and move back in with her husband. And my mother moved in with them again. It was when she was 18 that she made an effort to go back to her mother, and her mother agreed. She agreed to "take her back in," as my mother put it. My mother forgave her everything. She was happy simply to belong to a family again, even though she never completely forgot the heedlessness her mother had shown towards her. The turmoil of wartime was not a sufficient excuse. Yet, despite all that, when, fifty years later, my grandmother—who was having more and more difficulty taking care of herself—had to move out of the modest apartment that she lived in, located in a run-down street in the Barbès neighborhood in the heart of the most working class part of Paris's 18th district, it was my mother who found her a studio in Reims and took care of her. A bit later, her physical deterioration having advanced to the point where she could barely move around on her own, she insisted on moving back to Paris for the final days of her life, and my mother found her an old people's home there. Her own resources were insufficient to pay the bills for this establishment, so until she died it was my mother and I who paid the bulk of the costs that social security wouldn't cover.

For many years I knew nothing, or next to nothing, about the story of my mother's life during and immediately after the war. During my childhood and my adolescence, in the 60s and 70s, I was very fond of my grandmother. She lived in Paris in those years. (In fact for me she had always lived in Paris, a city she loved. She had been intent on going to live there in the mid-1950s, and had left her husband in Reims in order to do so.) She worked managing an apartment building, first in the 13th district (rue Pascal), then in one of the narrow streets around *les Halles* (the rue Tiquetonne, which these days has been utterly trans-formed). Later she would manage a building in a more middle-class neighborhood in the 12th district (on the rue Taine) before finally retiring and moving into her apartment in Barbès. She lived with a different man, whom I always called "grandpa"—one's real family and one's biological family (not to mention one's legal family) coincide much less frequently than is commonly assumed, and versions of what in the 1990s came regularly to be called "blended families" existed long before then. In this working-class world, marital and familial structures had for a very long time—both for better and for worse—been marked by complexity, multiplicity, by break-ups, serial part-nerships, reorganizations, etc. (There were couples who were simply "shacked up," there were children of different marriages mixed together, there were married men and women living together without having divorced their previous spouses.) My grandmother and her newest companion never got married. And my grandmother never divorced the man she married in 1946, who only died in the 1970s or 80s, without her having seen him in many years. During my teenage years (and indeed much later), I felt embarrassed by this somewhat "irregular" familial situation. The result was that I would lie about the ages of my grandmother and my mother so that people couldn't figure out that my grandmother was only 17 when my mother was born. I would also speak as if the man I called my grandfather was in fact the second husband of my grandmother. The social order puts pressure on all of us. All those people who want things to be "regular," or "meaningful," or to correspond to "stable points of reference" know they can count on the way adherence to the norm is inculcated into the deepest levels of our consciousness from our earliest years. This happens by way of our ongoing experience of the social world and by way of the discomfort— the shame—we come to feel when the part of the world in which we live fails to follow those tidily organized political and legal rules. The surrounding culture offers us those rules both as the only way life can be lived and as an ideal we must strive for. This is the case even if any such version of a normative family or familial norm in fact corresponds to nothing we ever encounter in real life. Surely the disgust I feel these days for all those people who wish to impose their definition of a couple, or a family, on us, or who would accord social and legal legitimacy to some among us and refuse it to others—such people regularly aim to achieve their ends by invoking models that have never existed except within the confines of their conservative and authoritarian imaginations—surely my disgust owes much of its intensity to my past, in which anyone inhabiting these alternative family forms was required to live in them and to experience them as somehow deviant or abnormal, and thus inferior and shameful. But this same past surely also explains my distrust of the opposite kind of injunction, an injunction to be abnormal, one that is directed at us by the advocates—in the end, just as profoundly normative in their own way—of non-normativity as a kind of prescribed "subversion." All my life, I have been well positioned to notice to what an extent normality and abnormality are realities that are not only relative, but also relational, mobile, contextual, the one always imbricated in the other, always partial in some way, and so on. I also cannot help having noticed to what an extent social illegitimacy can cause psychic damage to those whose lives are caught up in it, full of worry and pain, and how it can thus engender a deeply rooted aspiration to gain access to the space of what is legitimate and what is "normal." (The power of certain institutions resides precisely in this kind of desirability.)[1]

The grandfather I knew in the 1960s (and I'm not putting any quotation marks around the word grandfather, because he really was my grandfather, to the extent that a family, whether or not it conforms legally to the decrees of the guardians of the social order, is always the result of an exercise of will and of decisions people have made, as well as, in every case, of the actual practice of the people concerned) was a window washer. He got around on a moped with his ladder and bucket, and would head out and wash the windows of cafés and businesses often located quite far from where he lived. One day as I was walking in central Paris and he was passing by, he saw me and stopped at the curb, delighted by this fortuitous meeting. I, on the other hand, was acutely embarrassed, terrified that someone I knew might see me with him, perched on top of his strange contraption. What would I have said if someone had asked me, "Who was that fellow you were chatting with?" Over the course of the next few days, I wrestled unsuccessfully with a terribly guilty conscience. "Why," I kept asking myself, "can't you just be who you are? What is it about the time spent in a bourgeois or petty bourgeois world that has led you to the point where you would be willing to deny your family or feel so ashamed of it? Why have you interiorized to such an extent all the hierarchies of the social world that, intellectually and politically, you claim to be opposed to?" But at the same time part of me would be cursing my family for being what it was: "What bad luck to have been born into those circumstances," I kept repeating to myself. I would alternate back and forth between these two positions, first blaming myself, then blaming them. (But whose fault was it, really? And what was their fault?) I was torn, ill at ease with myself. My political convictions didn't mesh with my attempt to fit in to the bourgeois world; the critical position I claimed to hold vis-à-vis the social world conflicted with certain values that were being imposed on me—and I can't even say it was despite myself, since I was under no obligation to assume these values. No obligation, that is, except for my voluntary submission to the perceptions and judgments of the dominant class. Politically, I was on the side of the workers, yet I detested being tied to their world. Doubtless I would have suffered fewer inner torments and less of a moral crisis in claiming allegiance to the "people," if those people hadn't been my family, which is to say my past, and therefore, whether I liked it or not, my present.

My grandfather drank a lot. ("He really likes his drink," people said of him.) After a few glasses of cheap red wine, he would launch into endless rants, demonstrating a linguistic inventiveness that was typical of working class speech of the time and that has an equivalent today in the kind of speech one can hear in teenagers from working-class suburbs. He wasn't ignorant. He knew a good deal about many different things, and imagined he knew a lot more than he did. This meant he never hesitated to put forth a firm opinion—one that was as often as not incorrect. He was a communist in the same way that bourgeois people find themselves on the right— it went without saying, it was the natural course of things, practically in the genes of someone who had been born into the working class. In this, he was like my father (until my father stopped being communist, and even after that, because there was a way in which even then he still remained a communist), beginning his sentences with "We workers…" One day, he described to me how he had been driving down the Boulevard Saint-Germain at 5 in the morning, and a group of drunk bourgeois types, leaving a party or a night club and walking down the middle of the street had screamed at him: "Filthy beggar!" When he spoke of the class struggle, it meant something quite concrete to him. He would dream out loud of the coming revolution. When I moved to Paris, I got into the habit of having Sunday lunch with my grandmother and him quite regularly. Sometimes my parents would come from Reims to join us and occasionally they would bring along my two younger brothers. But I would have been mortified if anyone I knew, or, a bit later, anyone I worked with, had found out exactly where they lived. I was quite discreet about this; when people asked me questions, I would be evasive or else tell outright lies.

It was obvious to me that there was some kind of tension between my mother and my grandmother, but it was only after my grandmother's death that I learned the reasons for it. At that point, my mother was eager to tell me what until then she had more or less kept quiet about: her abandonment, the orphanage, her mother's refusal to take care of her after the war. My mother had never spoken to anyone about any of this. "My subconscious had kept it hidden," she said, making odd use of some psychoanalytic lingo she must have heard on television. But clearly this was something that she had always remembered, while preferring to keep it to herself, even if it couldn't help but slip out a bit from time to time. (For instance, when, as a child I would complain about something or other, she would sometimes yell at me, "Maybe you'd prefer to grow up in an orphanage?") But then she added something else to the story she told me, making it seem as if a family's history was nothing other than a successive series of shameful events, one hiding inside the next, and none of them spoken about either inside or outside the family. This revelation made the picture she had been painting seem even a shade darker than it had already appeared. Even she had known nothing about this until her brother told her while explaining why he refused to pay any part of his mother's nursing home expenses. Along with reminding her of how their mother had abandoned them, he told her about other events that up till then she hadn't known about. My mother didn't repeat these stories to me until months later, after their mother was dead. She must have suddenly felt free to tell me, all in one go, both what she had always hidden from us about her childhood and what she had just learned about her own mother. It made me think again about the strange woman my grandmother had been. In spite of her kindness, there was also a harshness in her that one could see in her eyes, and that sometimes snuck out in the tone of her voice. Perhaps this is because she had never forgotten that terrible day: how she was screamed at, beaten perhaps. And never forgotten the weeks that followed, the time it took for her hair to grow back, for the neighbors finally to stop thinking about it, for it to shrink down to the size of a rumor that would only pop up from time to time in conversations about her. She "liked to have a good time." If I understand the expression my mother used about her correctly, it means that she liked to live as a free woman, to go out at night and have fun, that she liked having sex with different men without feeling the need to become attached or to stay together with them for too long. Her children were probably, for her, an annoyance, and motherhood something she had to put up with rather than something she chose. At the time, contraception was hard to come by. An abortion could land you in prison. In fact, she spent time in prison after the war for having had an abortion. How long was she in prison? I don't know, nor does my mother. Men were certainly free to exercise their sexuality as they liked, but not women. Doubtless in working class environments there was a certain kind of sexual freedom available, or, at the least, freedom when compared to the rules laid out by bourgeois morality—the very freedom that would have caused the defenders of bourgeois morality to denounce the dissolute lives of those who enjoyed living by other rules. But for women, the choice to live freely was risky in many different ways.

So what happened after the armistice was signed in 1940 and the region was occupied by the German army? It wasn't just that my grandmother, 27 years old, went voluntarily to work in Germany. She was also accused—was it true or wasn't it?—of having an affair with a German officer. I can imagine something of what might have been going on: her desire to survive, to have food to eat, not to be poor or to have to endure the food shortages. Who was this enemy soldier? Did she love him? Or was she simply trying to obtain a better standard of living than the one she had had up till then? One possibility doesn't, of course, exclude the other. And then how did she come to the decision to abandon not only her children, but also her partner? I won't ever be able to answer these questions. Just as I'll never know what it felt like for her to have to endure the consequences of her choices, becoming like the "victim" in the "the ripped frock," the "hapless one who lay still on the paving stone," "uncrowned" and "disfigured," about whom Éluard writes with compassion in a famous poem, a poem of sadness and of "remorse."[2]

2

SO IT WAS THAT WHEN the Liberation came my grandmother met the fate of that group of women who hadn't managed to foresee the significance and the consequences of their actions. Was she all alone in that moment, one that must have seemed to her to last an "eternity," when she was subjected to "the exercise of a hasty, ridiculous justice" (to cite Marguerite Duras's words in *Hiroshima mon amour*), when she was subjected to "the ultimate of horror and stupidity"?[3] Or perhaps it took place during one of those scenes of collective punishment, images of which are sometimes found in documentaries about the end of the war, where one sees groups of women obliged to parade through a jeering crowd, insulted and spat upon? I don't know and my mother didn't tell me any more about it. In fact she told me there was nothing else she knew, nothing except for the basic, brutal fact of the matter. Her brother had told her that their mother's head had been shaved. Having lived through defeat and the Occupation, the French nation reasserted its virility by punishing women for their sexual misbehavior, real or imagined, by reasserting masculine power over women.[4]

Ever since I learned about this, each time I happen upon photographs of one of these scenes of humiliation—knowing, as we do, that so many highly placed collaborators, in so many middle-class circles, for instance, never had to experience this kind of opprobrium, or any loss of status, or the violence of public condemnation—, I can't help looking to see if there is any indication of where the photo was taken, and asking myself if perhaps my grandmother isn't one of the people pictured. Is one of those distraught faces or terrified gazes hers? How did she ever manage to forget what was done to her? How long did it take her to "come out of eternity" (Duras again)? Of course I would have preferred to learn that she had been in the Resistance, that she had endangered her own life by hiding Jews, or simply that she had sabotaged components in the factory where she was working—or anything else that one could be proud of. We always dream of having a glorious family, whatever kind of glory it might be. But there is no changing the past. The best you can do is to ask yourself: what can be made of this history of which I am so ashamed? What can be done with these past horrors when there is no getting around the fact that, no matter what you do, no matter what happens, this really is your ancestry? Could I simply take refuge in imagining that this history, given that I only learned about it recently, held no significance for me? (But suppose I had known of it? What would I have thought of my grandmother? Would I have dared ask her about it? Asking myself these questions upsets me even today.) Yet this whole series of events—my grandmother abandoning her children, her stay in Germany, etc.—had such an impact on my mother's life, on the shape of her personality and her subjectivity, that it's impossible not to conclude that it must therefore also have had a huge impact on my early years, and on those that would follow.

All of this serves to explain why my mother never continued her schooling, a fact that upsets her still today. "It's because my mother and I were both cursed," she suggests in order to explain all these misfortunes, all this distress. This inner conflict has remained with her throughout her life: she could have become something other than that for which she was intended had the war not brutally destroyed all her childhood dreams. Knowing perfectly well how intelligent she is, she has never been able to accept this injustice. And one of the major effects of this fate was that she was never able to aspire to "find someone better" than my father. But social endogamy is as rigidly controlled as is academic success. The laws governing the two processes are tightly intertwined. She has never given up thinking—even today—that she could have become an "intellectual" and met "someone more intelligent." But she was a cleaning lady, and she met a worker who, like her, had not been lucky enough to stay in school, and who, on top of all that, was not particularly open minded.

In 1950, at the age of twenty, she married the young man who was to become my father. They had two children in the next few years, my older brother and me. We were extremely poor, nearly destitute. So as not to make matters any worse, my mother decided not to have any more children, and therefore had no other choice than to have, I believe, several abortions. They were clandestine abortions, of course, and thus dangerous in every way—both legally and medically. (I remember my parents traveling one day to a town outside of Paris, Juvisy-sur-Orge. The preparations for the trip, as well as the trip itself, seemed very mysterious. I remember the worry written on my mother's face, my father's silence. Once in Paris, they dropped me and my brother at my grandmother's. Several hours later they returned, and my mother, elliptically and in a low voice, explained to my grandmother that everything had gone well. My brother and I were quite young at the time and yet, strangely enough, we knew what was going on. Or is it that I have the impression that we always knew, whereas I only understood it later but have super-imposed that understanding on my memories of the earlier moment?) My parents would, in the end, have two other children, but later, eight and fourteen years after my birth.

It was quite soon after her marriage that my mother became able to feel for her husband nothing but a constant sense of hostility, a sense that found its expression in shouting matches, the slamming of doors, or the shattering of dishes on the floor during their frequent arguments. It found more profound expression in nearly every moment of their daily life together. Their relationship seemed to be one long, continuous domestic dispute, as if the only way they knew how to speak to each other was by hurling at each other the most painful and damaging terms of abuse they could think of. On a number of occasions, she decided to divorce him. She went to see a lawyer who urged her not to leave before any official decision was pronounced. Otherwise, she would put herself in the wrong (for "deserting the marital home") and would lose custody of her children. She worried about my father becoming violent once he learned what she was planning, and about the "living hell" she would have to endure for the months (or even years) the legal procedure—which would also be costly—would take. She also worried that she wouldn't be able to "make it" on her own, and so to avoid "depriving" her "kids" of anything, she gave up the idea. Their routine went on: arguments, shouting, the trading of insults, just as before. Detesting your partner became a way of life. It was quite different from what Stanley Cavell calls "the conversation of marriage," or, in any case, it was a sad and strange version of that model.[5]

Still, it's important not to impose too quickly on her situation an insufficiently nuanced vision built on a certain kind of feminist framework, since that would hide part of the truth. (Feminism, which enables us to see and understand so many things, could in this case become a kind of epistemological obstacle.) For my mother was quite violent, perhaps, in reality, even more violent than my father. In fact, in the one physical confrontation between them that I know of, it was she who injured him by throwing at him the handle of the electric mixer she was using to make soup. It hit him hard enough to break two of his ribs. And, as it turns out, she was quite proud of this feat of strength, since she recounted it to me in the way one tells of a sporting triumph. It was proof in her eyes that she never let herself be taken advantage of. Still, whoever was in the right or in the wrong, the atmosphere was a harsh one, painful on a daily basis, even unbearable. This constant climate of conjugal warfare, these repeated scenes of verbal confrontation, the yelling, the shared madness, all with the children as witnesses, must have counted for a lot in producing my will to flee both my family and my circumstances (and for the longest time to wish to escape even from the idea of a family, of a couple, of married life, of a long-term relationship, of living together with someone, all of which horrified me).

It was thanks to my mother that I was able to attend high school, and to continue my education. She never put it in so many words, but I believe that she saw in me someone she could help to have the chance she had never had. The dreams she had been forced to abandon could be realized through me. But the process reawakened many old forms of sadness and resentment that had remained hidden in the depths of her soul. When I had just entered sixth grade, we learned a little Christmas rhyme in my English class. When I got home, I told my mother (I was 11 years old): "I learned a poem," and I began reciting it to her in English. I still remember it: "I wish you a merry Christmas, a horse and a gig, and a good fat pig, to kill next year." Her anger, her fury even, burst out before I had even finished. Was it that she thought I was trying to make fun of her? To make her feel small? To show my superiority over her now that I had finished my first few months of secondary education? She began screaming like a madwoman: "You know I don't speak any English! Translate what you said to me right now!" I translated. It was over in a moment; the hysterical crisis lasted only a brief instant. But from that point on I became aware that a divide now existed— and it would, of course, only grow wider—between the outside, represented by middle school and high school, by what I was learning, and the inside, which is to say, our home.

All my mother's frustration at not having been able to stay in school expressed itself in that outburst of anger. It would appear again and again in the following years, in many different ways. All it would take was a small critical observation or the slightest expression of disagreement for me to be upbraided: "Just because you're in high school doesn't mean you're any more important than we are," or "Who do you think you are? You think you're better than us?" I don't know how many times she felt obliged to remind me that "you're no different than the rest of us." But the words that came back the most frequently were the simple reminder that she had been denied what I was receiving: "I never got to…" or "No one ever gave me…" Yet, unlike my father, who was always reminding us about what had been denied to him as part of his astonishment that it wasn't being denied to his children (and sometimes as part of his own effort to deny it to them), when my mother's resentment found expression it was part of her way of admitting that I was going to have options that she had never had, or that had been foreclosed before she had more than a glimpse of them. She wanted to be sure I knew how lucky I was. When she would say, "I never had …," what she meant was, "You should know what it means that you get to …"

When she did try to take up her studies again, it was a huge disappointment. She had come across an advertisement in the regional newspaper. A new private school had opened—it was probably some kind of a scam, or at the very least the project of some quite unscrupulous people—that claimed to offer courses in computers to adults who wanted to retrain themselves for new careers and new professions. She signed up, paid a lot of money to attend classes several nights a week after work, only to quickly realize that she wasn't understanding a thing. She stuck with it—stubbornly. For several weeks she insisted that there was no way she would quit, that she was going to catch up. But finally she admitted the inevitable, and gave up in defeat. The defeat was a bitter and galling one. She had just watched her last chance disappear.

Having cleaned houses for years, my mother stopped working after my youngest brother was born, in 1967. But that didn't last. Economic pressures forced her to look for a job, and so she began working eight exhausting hours a day in a factory (the single month I spent there during the summer vacation after I took the Baccalaureate exam allowed me to experience what such an "occupation" was really like), all so that I would be able to take courses on Montaigne and Balzac in high school or, once I started university, so that I could spend hours holed up in my room struggling through Aristotle and Kant. While she was sleeping at night in order to get up at 4 a.m., I was staying up till dawn reading Marx and Trotsky, then Beauvoir and Genet. Annie Ernaux expressed the brutal truth of this situation with great simplicity, writing about her mother, who ran a small neighborhood grocery store: "I was both certain of her love for me and aware of one blatant injustice: she spent all day selling milk and potatoes so that I could sit in a lecture hall and learn about Plato."[6] As I look at my mother today, her body stiffened and painful as a result of the harsh tasks she performed for nearly fifteen years, standing on an assembly line attaching tops to glass jars, with only one ten-minute bathroom break each morning and another in the afternoon, I can't help but be struck by what social inequality means concretely, physically. Even the very word "inequality" seems to me to be a euphemism that papers over the reality of the situation, the naked violence of exploitation. A worker's body, as it ages, reveals to anyone who looks at it the truth about the existence of classes. It is nearly impossible to imagine the pace of the work flow in that factory—in most factories, really. One day an inspector had timed one worker for a few minutes, and that measurement determined the quota of jars that needed to be finished in an hour. It was already unimaginable, inhuman. And yet then you must consider that a good portion of their salary was tied to bonuses that were linked to the total number of jars finished in a day. My mother told me that she and her colleagues would sometimes manage to double the required number. She'd come home at night exhausted, "done in," as she'd say, but still pleased to have earned that day enough for us to maintain a decent standard of living. It is impossible for me to understand how and why the issue of harsh working conditions and all the slogans that denounced them— "Slow down the assembly lines!" [À bas les cadences infernales]—have disappeared from discourse on the left, and even from its perception of the social world. Because after all, what are at stake are the most concrete realities of many individual lives—people's very health, for example.

Back when I was young, to be honest, I wasn't so concerned about the implacable harshness of the conditions of factory work—or I was concerned only in an abstract kind of way. I was too fascinated by all I was discovering about culture, about literature, about philosophy to spend time thinking about what was going into making my access to these things possible. Indeed, it was quite the opposite: I resented my parents for being who they were, for not being the interlocutors of my dreams, or the kinds of interlocutors some of my fellow students had in their parents.

Being the first in my family to embark on an upward trajectory, I had little inclination, as a teenager, to try to understand who they were, and even less inclination to understand and assimilate on a political level the truth of their existence. I may have been a Marxist, but I have to say that my Marxism, like my engagement on the left, was perhaps little more than a way of idealizing the working class, of transforming it into a mythical entity compared to which the actual life of my parents seemed utterly reprehensible. They were eager to get their hands on all the products consumer society was making available and all I could see in the sorry state of their daily life and in their aspiration for forms of comfort that had long been denied them was the sign of their social "alienation" and of their misplaced aspirations to join the middle class. They were workers and they had lived in poverty. Like everyone in my family, like all our neighbors, like everyone we knew, they were eager to obtain everything that had been denied them up till now, everything that had been denied to their parents before them. As soon as they were able to, they would buy what they had been dreaming of, even if it was on credit: a used car, then a new car, a television, furniture from a catalogue (a Formica table for the kitchen, a sofa in artificial leather for the living room, and so on). I found it deplorable that they were constantly caught in the grip of this desire for material well-being, that they became envious of others—"If they have it, there's no reason we shouldn't have it too." It was unpleasant for me to realize that perhaps these desires and this envy had been what determined their political choices, even if they would not themselves have made a link between these two different registers. In my family, everyone bragged about how much this or that item had cost, because it showed they weren't in need, that they had made it. Feelings of pride and honor were tightly linked with a regular habit of announcing what everything had cost. This hardly matched up with the heroic stories of the "worker's movement" with which my head was filled. But what is the point of a political story that doesn't take into account what people are really like as it interprets their lives, a story whose result is that one ends up blaming the individuals in question for not conforming to the fiction one has constructed? It is clearly a story that needs to be rewritten in order to make it less unified and less simple, to build in more complexity and more contradictions. And to reintroduce historical time. The working class changes. It doesn't stay identical to itself. And clearly the working class of the 1960s and 1970s was no longer the same as that of the 1930s or the 1950s. The same position in the social field does not correspond to exactly the same realities, nor to the same aspirations.[7]

My mother recently reminded me, with more than a touch of irony in her voice, that I was always criticizing them for being too "bourgeois." ("You were always saying stupid things like that in those days," she added. "I hope at least now you are aware of it.") Basically, according to the way I looked at things back then, my parents were betraying whatever it was that they were supposed to go on being, and my disdain for them was simply the expression of my desire certainly to be nothing like them— and even more certainly to be nothing like what it was that I wanted them to be. For me, the "proletariat" was an idea that came straight out of a book, something abstract. My parents didn't fit the image. I may have been keeping myself amused and entertained by deploring the distance separating a class "in itself" from a class "for itself," separating the "alienated worker" from a "class consciousness," but the truth is that this "revolutionary" political position simply served as a cover for the social judgment that I had passed on my parents and my family, for my desire to escape from their world. My youthful Marxism was thus a vector for a kind of social disidentification: I glorified the "working class" in order to put more distance between myself and actual workers. While reading Marx and Trotsky, I imagined myself at the avant-garde of the people. But really I was finding my way into a world of people of privilege, into their kind of temporality, their modes of subjectivation: the world of people who had the leisure time available for reading Marx and Trotsky. I was fascinated by Sartre's writings about the working class, but I was repulsed by the working class in which I was immersed, by the working class environment that limited my horizons. To be interested in Marx or Sartre was my way of getting out of this world, out of my parents' world, all the while of course imagining that I was more clear sighted than they were about their own lives. My father was perfectly aware of this. I had begun to read *Le Monde*—one of the ways in which I was forever putting on display my deeply serious interest in politics. Not quite knowing how to give voice to the hostility he felt towards this newspaper— it was clearly not intended for people like him, he felt; it was in his eyes a vehicle for middle-class ideology (he was better informed than I was!)—he simply declared, in a voice full of anger: "Nobody but schoolmarms reads that rag." [C'est un journal de curé que tu es en train de lire.] Then he got up and walked out of the room.

My mother didn't have a very clear idea about what was going on in my life, about what I was getting up to. I had entered a different world, one in which everything seemed far off and unfamiliar to her. And then I hardly ever spoke to her about my interests, since she had no idea who these authors were that I found so fascinating. Once, when I was about 15 or 16, she picked up a novel by Sartre that was lying on my desk and commented a bit hesitantly, "I think this book is a bit crude." It was an opinion she had heard from a woman whose house she cleaned—someone from the middle class in whose eyes Sartre must have been some kind of dangerous writer—and she repeated it a bit naively, perhaps as a way of showing me that she knew at least the name of one of the authors I was reading.

One thing, at least, was sure: I didn't match the image she had of someone who was "pursuing their education." In high school, I was active in a group of extreme leftists, and that took up a lot of my time. The principal even called in my father to tell him about my "propagandistic" activities at the entrance to, and even inside the school. The scene that followed at home that evening was dramatic: they threatened to take me out of school. My mother was worried that I would fail the Baccalaureate exam, but above all, she and my father had a great deal of difficulty accepting that I wasn't devoting all of my time to studying, since they were wearing themselves thin in order to give me the opportunity to do precisely that. They were both furious and disgusted. I was given an ultimatum: either drop the political activism or drop out of school. I declared that I would prefer to drop out of school. That was the last I heard of the matter. When it came right down to it, my mother was too deeply invested in the idea that I continue.

As for my studies, there too, I failed to conform to what she had in mind. My choice to study philosophy must have seemed ludicrous to her. She barely knew what to say when I told her of my decision. She would have preferred that I choose to study English or Spanish. (Medicine or Law would never have occurred to her—or to me—, whereas choosing a language was for her the best way to guarantee myself a future as a high school teacher.) But above all she was aware of the distance that was being established between us. I was becoming incomprehensible to her, and she readily commented that I seemed "eccentric." I can imagine how strange I must have seemed to her, how bizarre. I was moving further and further away from what was, in her eyes, the normal world, a normal life. "But it's just not normal to …" were words she often repeated about me, as did my father.

"Not normal," "strange," "bizarre." It's nonetheless the case that such words still contained no direct or indirect reference to sexuality, even if my parents' perception of me was, of course, connected to the style I was taking up, the general image I wanted to give of myself. My hair was quite long, and that drove my father crazy for many years. ("Go get a haircut right now," he would shout, pounding on the table.) Doubtless the sexual dissidence that I would soon assert was already legible in that style and that image. But it would only be years later that my mother discovered I belonged to the category that she could only manage to refer to as "people like you." Her desire not to employ any vocabulary that might be taken as derogatory and her uncertainty as to how to do this meant that she could think of no word she could safely use, and so resorted to this awkward circumlocution. Quite recently, when, looking at a photograph she had at her house, I asked her who the three young people in it were, she replied: "Those are the children of B.," which is to say my older brother's partner. She went on, "The one in the middle is D. He's like you." At first I didn't understand what she meant, but then she added, "When he told his mother he was ... you know ... you see what I mean ... that he was like you ... she kicked him out. But then your brother made her change her mind by pointing out that if that's how she felt, it would mean he could never invite his own brother to his house." I was surprised to hear that about my brother. As far as I could remember, he hadn't always been so tolerant. It appeared his views had changed considerably on this topic. But in point of fact, I never do visit him at his house. I've never tried to visit. I've never wanted to visit ... And as this whole book is trying to demonstrate, this is due to my social identity, my class identity, as much as or more than it is due to my sexual identity. If it is now the case that he accepts who I am and yet I haven't gotten back in touch, it's obviously because I am uncomfortable with who he is. I thus have to admit that if, these days, we still never see each other, it is more because of me than because of him. It is not so easy to overcome the past. Trajectories that have diverged to this degree do not easily come back together.

Yet this is also an example of the truth of something Bourdieu demonstrated about the family: that it is not some stable entity, but rather a set of strategies. Say my brothers had become lawyers, university professors, journalists, high-ranking government officials, artists, writers ... We would still be in touch, even if in some distant kind of way, and in any case, I would have claimed them as brothers, accepted them as such. The same is true for my aunts and uncles, cousins, nieces and nephews ... If one's available social capital is, first of all, the set of family relations one maintains and can bring into play, it could be said that my trajectory—with all the ruptures it involved—did not just endow me with an absence of social capital, it left me with a negative balance: I had to nullify certain relationships as opposed to maintaining them. This was a far cry from claiming distant cousins as my own, as happens in bourgeois families; in my case it was more a matter of cutting my own brothers out of my life. There thus was and would be no one I could count on to help me move forward along the paths I had chosen, to help me overcome any difficulties I might encounter.

When I was 18 or 20, my mother didn't yet take me to be one of those "people like you," but she nonetheless watched me change with an increasing sense of astonishment. She was at a loss for what to think. And I took no notice, since I had already more or less separated myself from her, from them, from their world.

3

AFTER THEIR MARRIAGE in 1950, my parents moved into a furnished room. Lodging was hard to come by in Reims in those years, so it was in that room that they spent the first years of their married life. They had two children, my older brother and me, and my grandfather made a wooden bed for the two of us in which we both slept, head to toe. We all lived together in that room until a social welfare organization arranged for my parents to move into a house in a new housing project for workers located on the other side of town. Really the word "house" isn't quite right: it was a cement block attached to other cement blocks, these blocks arranged on either side of a street that ran parallel to other similar streets. They were all one-story houses, with one main room and a bedroom (which the four of us therefore shared, just as we had before). There was no bathroom, but there was running water and a sink in the main room. The sink was thus used both for cooking and for bathing. In winter, the coal burning stove wasn't capable of heating the two rooms sufficiently, so we were chilled to the bone all of the time. There was a small yard adjoined to the house, offering a touch of greenery, and my father managed with great pains to grow a few vegetables in it for us.

Have I retained any memories from those years? Rare ones, vague and uncertain. Except for one, that is, which is quite precise and quite haunting: it is of my father coming home dead drunk after having gone missing for two or three days. ("Every Friday night, after work, he would live it up in the bars," my mother told me, "and he often wouldn't come home.") He is standing at one end of the room and taking every bottle he could lay his hands on—oil, milk, wine—and throwing them one by one against the opposite wall, where they shatter. My brother and I are crying, huddled up against our mother, who is simply repeating, in a voice of both anger and despair, "at least watch out for the kids." When, shortly after my father's death, I reminded my mother of this scene and several others as part of an explanation for why I hadn't wanted to attend his funeral, she was astonished: "You can remember that? But you were so little." Yes, I could remember it. I had always remembered it. I had never been able to forget it. It was a kind of indelible trace left by a childhood trauma, linked to an "originary scene," but not one that should be understood in psychological or psychoanalytic terms. Once you start talking about the Oedipus complex, you desocialize and depoliticize the way you look at processes of subjectivation. A family scene replaces one that is grounded in historical and geographical (urban) reality, which is to say the reality of social classes. What was going on here was not the weakening of the paternal imago, not a failure to identify with the father—real or symbolic; it corresponds to neither of these interpretative schemas, the ones that would be routinely invoked by habitual forms of Lacanian thought in order to discover the "key" to my homosexuality—a "key" they plant there ahead of time in order to be able to discover it. No, there is no fodder here that anyone can use to trot out yet again these notions that have been fabricated by psychoanalytic ideology and that its proselytizers are constantly repeating.[8] What was going here was rather what I would call a social mirror stage, one in which someone becomes conscious of belonging to a milieu in which certain kinds of behaviors and practices occur; this was a scene of interpellation, but a social, not a psychic or an ideological one; it was an interpellation involving the discovery of a class-based sociological situation, one that assigns to you a place and to an identity; it teaches you to recognize who you are and who you will be by means of an image someone else presents—someone else whom you are meant to become. But in fact it turns out that what was planted in me in that moment was rather a patient and obstinate desire to contradict the future for which I was intended. Yet at the same time I was left with a lasting impression of my social origin, a call to "remember where you came from" that no later transformation, no cultural education, no disguise, no subterfuge, would ever allow me to forget. That, at least, is the meaning that, retrospectively, it seems to me possible to give to this moment from my distant past, even if I realize that this is a reconstruction—as any other interpretation would be, including, of course, a psychoanalytic one. The processes by which you come to belong to yourself or to transform yourself, to constitute an identity or to refuse an identity, were thus always tightly linked for me, imbricated each one in the other, fighting with each other, holding each other in check. My most basic social identification (recognizing oneself as oneself) was thus from the outset perturbed by a disidentification that fed constantly on the very identification being refused.

I always held it against my father that he was the man he was, the incarnation of a certain kind of working class world that, unless you had belonged to it and lived in it at some point, you could only ever encounter in books or at the movies: "It was like some-thing straight out of a Zola novel," my mother once said to me, without ever having read a page of Zola. Even if you have belonged to that world or known that past, it can be difficult to accept them and take them on as your own. I'm painfully aware that the way I have arranged the writing of this book assumes—both about me and about my readers—that we are socially distant from the circumstances and from the people who still live the kinds of lives I am attempting to describe and to reconstruct. I am equally aware how improbable it is that any of those people could end up reading these pages. When people write about the working class world, which they rarely do, it is most often because they have left it behind. They thereby contribute to perpetuating the social illegitimacy of the people they are speaking of in the very moment of speaking about them. This happens even if they write with the goal of exposing and critiquing the very status of social illegitimacy to which these people are relegated over and over again, because in writing they take a necessary critical dis-tance, and with it comes the position of a judge or an evaluator.

When you get right down to it, it wasn't so much the person who had committed these acts who horrified me, it was more the social scene in which such acts were possible. The breaking of the bottles couldn't have lasted more than a few minutes, and yet I believe that it established in me a disgust at this impoverishment, a refusal to accept the fate that had been meted out to me, and a secret feeling of woundedness, a wound that is still painful, related to having always to bear the burden of this memory. And in fact, such episodes were hardly rare. I must have been 4 or 5, and my father 27 or 28. He was having difficulty giving up a certain kind of (mostly male) working class sociability, one he had only discovered upon becoming an adult: nights spent drinking with your buddies, time spent in bars after work. And since it sometimes happened that he wouldn't come home for several days, it seems likely he must have spent some of these nights with other women. He had married at the age of 21, and three years later he already had two children. He must have been eager for an occasional break from the obligations of married life and of parenthood, for a chance to experience the distractions of youthful freedom. I imagine he must have wanted to enjoy all those things that had been denied him by his family situation and by all the responsibilities associated with it that were weighing him down. He had moved directly from being an oldest son with serious family obligations to being a husband and father with serious family obligations. It must have been hard to bear, just as it must have been difficult to face up to the fact that all the rest of his life was going to be similarly constrained by familial duties. His disorderly conduct (a phrase whose negative connotations hardly do justice to the complexity of the whole situation it designates) also needs to be understood as a way of giving himself a little breathing space—and a little pleasure. Obviously, no similar behavior was possible—it would have been unthinkable—for my mother, who was obliged to take care of the children on her own. And in any case, my father would never have permitted her to spend her time in cafés, not to mention not coming home at night. (For that he would have killed her, after having broken everything in the house!)

So as the child of a worker you experience in your very flesh the sense of belonging to the working class. When I was writing my book about the conservative revolution in France, I checked several books by Raymond Aron out of the library. The ideologues who, during the 1980s and 1990s, had it in mind to impose the hegemony of right wing forms of thought on French intellectual life at that time quite reasonably claimed to be his followers. As I skimmed over a few samples of the shallow, lifeless prose of this pompous and tedious professor, I came across the following sentence: "If I make an effort to remember my 'class consciousness' from before I began studying sociology, it is barely possible for me to do so without the gap of the intervening years seeming to me to render the object indistinct; to put this another way, it does not seem to me to have been established that every member of a modern society has the sense of belonging to a clearly defined group, one called a class, that exists within the larger social whole. The objective reality of society's stratification into groups is undeniable, but that of classes conscious of themselves is not."[9]

What strikes me as particularly undeniable is that the absence of the feeling of belonging to a class is characteristic of children of the bourgeoisie. People in a dominant class position do not notice that they are positioned, situated, within a specific world (just as someone who is white isn't necessarily aware of being so, or someone heterosexual). Read in this light, Aron's remark can be seen for what it is, the naive confession offered by a person of privilege who imagines he is writing sociology when all he is doing is describing his own social status. I only met him once in my life, and immediately felt a strong aversion towards him. The very moment I set eyes on him, I loathed his ingratiating smile, his soothing voice, his way of demonstrating how reasonable and rational he was, everything about him that displayed his bourgeois *ethos* of decorum and propriety, of ideological moderation. (In reality, his writings are filled with a violence that those at whom it is directed would not be able to avoid feeling were they ever to come across it. It suffices to read—but there are other choices too—the pages he wrote about the working-class strikes in the 1950s. People have praised his lucidity because he was anticommunist while others still blindly supported the Soviet Union. But this is wrong! He was anticommunist because of his hatred of the working class, and he set himself up as the political and ideological defender of the bourgeois establishment, defending against anything having to do with the aspirations or the political activities of the working class. Basically, his pen was for hire: he was a soldier in the service of those in power helping them to maintain their power. Sartre was right a thousand times over to insult him in May 1968. Aron had more than earned it. Let us salute the greatness of Sartre for daring to break with the conventions of polite academic "discussion"— which always works in favor of "orthodoxy," and its reliance on "common sense" and what seems "self-evident" in its opposition to heterodoxy and to critical thought. Sartre did this at a moment when it had become important to "insult those who are the real insulters," to recall a helpful reminder Genet offers us, a happy turn of phrase we should always be ready to take up as our motto.)

In my case, I can say that I have always deeply had the feeling of belonging to a class, which does not mean that the class I belonged to was conscious of itself as such. One can have the sense of belonging to a class without that class being aware of itself as such or being "a clearly defined group." It can still be a group whose reality, whatever else may be the case, is experienced in concrete situations of daily life. An example would be when my mother would take us, my brother and myself, with her to the houses she was cleaning on the days we didn't have school. While she worked, we would stay in the kitchen and would hear the woman employing her ask her to do this or that, or offer compliments or reproaches. (There was one day on which we heard her reproached: "I'm very disappointed; you just can't be trusted to do it right," and then saw her come back to the kitchen in tears. We were terrified to see her in such a state. Even today remembering that scene —and that horrible tone of voice!—what disgust I feel for a world in which insulting people comes as easily as breathing, what hatred has remained with me over the years for those kinds of power relations, those hierarchical structures!) I can't help imagining that there was a cleaning lady in the home Raymond Aron grew up in, and that when he saw her it never occurred to him that she was "conscious of belonging to a social group" that wasn't the one he belonged to; that he was taking tennis lessons while she ironed his shirts, washed the floor, and cleaned the bathrooms, following his mother's orders; that as he was following an educational trajectory leading to further study in prestigious places, her children, the same age as him, would soon be starting work at a factory, or had already done so. When I see photos from his childhood, with his family, what I see is the bourgeois world on display in all its self-satisfaction (a self-satisfaction of which it is surely fully conscious). And yet he is unaware of this? Even retrospectively? And can still call himself a sociologist?

When I was a child, my parents knew a couple in which the man was a worker in the wine cellars and the woman was a caretaker at a mansion in a rich part of town, lived in by one of the big families of the Champagne industry of the region. This couple lived in a lodge near the entrance gate to the mansion. Sometimes we would go visit them for Sunday lunch and I would play with their daughter in the yard in front of the impressive building. We knew that there was another world nearby, up the set of steps that led to the terrace before the front door, one that had an elaborate window above it. Of that other world we had only rare and fleeting glimpses: a fancy car pulling up, someone dressed in a way we had never seen before… Yet we knew without even having to think about it—it was immediately apparent to us—that there was a difference between "us" and "them," between, on the one hand, the occupants of this mansion and the friends who visited them, and, on the other, those who lived in the two or three rooms of the caretaker's lodge and the friends they would invite over on their days off, which is to say my parents, my brother, and me. How would it have been possible for us not to be aware of the fact that social classes existed, given how great the distance was between these two universes, separated by only a few dozen yards? Aware that classes existed, and that we belonged to one of them? Richard Hoggart is right to insist on the obviousness of the circumstances in which you live for anyone who belongs to the working class.[10] The difficulties of daily life recall them to you at every turn, as does the evident contrast with the living conditions of other people. How would it be possible not to know what you are, when you see how other people live and how different they are from you?

At the beginning of the 1960s, we went to live in a newly con-structed low-income housing complex, where, thanks to endless efforts on my mother's part, we had obtained an apartment. It was, I believe, a good example of public housing that has been integrated into the surrounding urban environment, and that is located in a central part of town: three different apartment "blocks," as they were called at the time, four stories high, and built in the middle of a neighborhood made up of individual houses. The neighborhood was located between an industrial area and the cellars of a number of the big Champagne houses (Taittinger, Mumm, Louis Roederer). The apartment had a dining room, a kitchen, and—at last!—two bedrooms, one for the parents and one for the children. Another novelty: we had a bathroom. I attended elementary school not far from there, and also went to a catechism class each Thursday at the Church of Saint Joan of Arc. Was that evidence of some strange paradoxical working class observance of religious tradition or simply a way of keeping children busy, and a form of child care, on the days when school wasn't in session? Probably both at the same time. My parents were not religious, and were even anticlerical. My father never set foot in a church; during familial ceremonies (baptisms, weddings, funerals, and so on) he remained outdoors with the other men while the women went inside. Still, they had made a point of having us baptized, and then of enrolling us in catechism classes— during which the priest, as one would expect, sat the boys on his lap and caressed their legs. (That was his reputation in the neighbor- hood, and I once heard my father proclaim his disgust for priests and their habits in this way: "If I find out that he's touched one of my kids, he won't know what hit him.") We continued with this reli- gious education up until our first communion, dressed in a white alb, with an enormous wooden crucifix hanging on our chests.

At my mother's place, I found some ridiculous photos of me and my brother from that day, taken with aunts, uncles, and cousins in front of my paternal grandfather's house. Everyone had gathered there after the ceremony for a festive lunch for which the religious ceremony doubtless provided an excuse or a pretext. Religious rituals, however absurd they may be, offer the occasion for gatherings that are quite pagan in nature, and that serve the function of keeping the family integrated, maintaining connections between brothers and sisters and establishing connections between their children—my cousins. These gatherings also simultaneously enable the reaffirmation of a certain social cohesion, since the cultural and professional homogeneity they evince is always total: no one has taken themselves out of the group since the previous family reunion. This must be what would later hold me back me from attending further ceremonies of this kind, notably the weddings of my two younger brothers: it was impossible for me to imagine myself once again immersed in these forms of sociability and culture, where I would now be so uncomfortable, taking part in the rituals that happen at the end of meals when everyone at the table calls out: "Simone, sing us a song!," "René, sing us a song!," and everyone has a song saved up that they sing on such occasions, maybe a comical one or a sentimental one. The same risqué jokes get told year after year, the same dances are danced, the same stupid comments that never seem to grow old are made, the same arguments break out as the night wears on, sometimes turning into fights as disagreements and points of discord from years gone by, often linked to suspicions of infidelity, rise once again to the surface.

Little has changed as regards the social homogeneity of my family. When I got to know my parents' house in Muizon, I examined the photos that were everywhere, on the walls and on top of various pieces of furniture. I would ask my mother who this or that person was. They were all part of the extended family: my brothers' children, a cousin and her husband, and so on. Each time I would ask, "What do they do?" The answers drew a map of today's working class: "He works in the X factory or the Y factory." "He works in the champagne cellars." "He's a builder." "He's in the National Guard." "He's out of work." The examples of social mobility occurred in the case of a female cousin who worked for the Internal Revenue Service or a sister-in-law who was a secretary somewhere. The intense poverty I knew in my childhood is no longer present: "They're not bad off," or "She earns a good salary," my mother would add after having told me the profession of the man or woman I was asking about. But the position occupied in the social field is still the same: an entire family group whose situation, whose relative position in the class structure, hasn't budged an inch.

A chapel in the Roman style designed by Léonard Foujita was being built only a few dozen yards from the building we were living in. He would decorate it with frescos to celebrate his conversion to Catholicism, which had happened in Reims in the Saint Remi Basilica a few years earlier. I would only learn about this much later: there wasn't much interest in art in our household, and even less for Christian art. I finally visited the chapel while I was writing this book. An interest in art is something that is learned. I learned it. It was part of my project of nearly complete self-reeducation, necessary in order to move into a different world, a different class—and to put some distance between myself and the world and the class from which I came. An interest in artistic and literary objects always ends up contributing, whether or not it happens consciously, to a way of defining yourself as having more self-worth; it helps produce a differentiation from those who lack access to those same objects, or a "distinction," in the sense of a gap between yourself and the others—those from an "inferior" or "uncultured" class. This distinction is constitutive of your sense of self and of the way you look at yourself. On so many occasions throughout the rest of my life as a "cultured" individual, I've had the chance to observe, while visiting an exhibition or attending a concert or an opera performance, to what an extent people who take part in "high" cultural practices seem to gain a sense of self-satisfaction from their participation in these activities, a feeling of superiority that can be read in the discreet smile that never leaves their lips, or in the way they hold themselves, the way they talk knowingly as connoisseurs, the way they display how at ease they are in these circumstances. All of these things are manners of expressing the social joy that results from corresponding to expectations, from belonging to the privileged world of those who can flatter themselves with appreciating "refined" forms of artistic expression. I was always intimidated by all of this, yet I went on trying to resemble these people, to act as if I was born into the same world they were, to appear as relaxed as they were in aesthetic situations.

It was also necessary to relearn how to talk, to eliminate incorrect pronunciations and turns of phrase along with regional usages (to stop saying that an apple was "sour" [*fière*] and say instead that it was "tart" [*acide*]), to correct both my northeastern accent and my working-class accent, to learn a more sophisticated vocabulary, to make use of more suitable grammatical constructions, in short, to keep both my language and my delivery of it under constant surveillance. "You talk like a book," I would often be told by members of my family as a way of making fun of my new habits while also indicating that they understood what I was up to. As time went by, and this is still the case today, I would in fact learn to be quite careful, when I found myself dealing with people whose language I had unlearned, not to make use of turns of phrase that seemed complicated or little used in popular circles. (For example, I might say "I'm gonna" instead of "I'll" [*j'ai été* instead of *je suis allé*]), and I would make an effort to return to the intonations, vocabulary, and idioms that, even if I've locked them away in a far corner of my memory and almost never use them, I've never forgotten. This isn't really a form of bilingualism, but more an interplay between two levels of language, two different social registers, both determined by one's situation and surroundings.

It was during the period in which we lived in that apartment that I started attending the city's "boy's high school." I really have to emphasize the fact that this was no ordinary kind of event within my family; in fact it was something new, a real break with the past. I was the first person to move on from primary to secondary education, even to the earliest stages of it. I was eleven years old, and my older brother, older by two years, hadn't gone to this school, but had remained in the primary schools. These two educational tracks existed side-by-side at the time, and this entailed a brutally direct screening process. A year later, my brother would become a butcher's apprentice. He wasn't interested in staying in school, finding it both boring and a waste of time. So my mother, having seen a small sign on the door of a butcher's shop that read "Apprentice needed," asked him if that was some-thing that would interest him. He said yes, so she took him to the shop and the matter was arranged. Thus did our trajectories begin to diverge, although in reality the origins of this divergence were probably to be found even further back. In very short order, everything about us was different, from our hair and our clothes to our ways of speaking and thinking. At the age of 15 or 16, all he wanted to do was hang out with his friends, play soccer, chat up the girls, and listen to Johnny Hallyday; I, on the other hand, wanted to stay at home and read, and my tastes went more in the direction of the Rolling Stones or Françoise Hardy (whose song "Tous les garçons et les filles de mon âge" seemed to have been written expressly to describe the loneliness of young gays), and then in the direction of Barbara and Léo Ferré, or Bob Dylan, Donovan, and Joan Baez—"intellectual" singers. My brother went on incarnating a working class ethos, a way of being and a set of bodily habits that kept him tightly knit to our social world, whereas I was constructing an equally typical ethos, that of a high school student. My choice put a distance between me and our world. (At 16, I was wearing a duffle-coat and Clarks Desert Boots and letting my hair grow long.) Even our relationship to politics set us apart from each other: he had no interest whatsoever in it, whereas from a young age I started going on and on about the "class struggle," a "permanent revolution," and the "international proletariat."

I was always terribly embarrassed when asked what my brother did and would inevitably find a way not to tell the truth. He observed my transformation into a young "intellectual" with a certain amount of disbelief and a good deal of irony. (What was also happening was my transformation into a young gay man, a fact which, of course, did not escape his notice. But coming from someone for whom incarnating the masculine values of the working class was so important, his sarcastic remarks were directed more at a general appearance and a style that struck him as "effeminate" than at a specific sexuality. The early signs and unsettling appeal of that sexuality were something I was myself only beginning to be aware of.) We were still living together, now in a large low-income housing project on the outskirts of the city. We had finally moved there in 1967. I was able to have my own room, because, high school student that I was, I needed it to study in. He shared his room with one of our younger brothers. The other, the youngest, slept in our parents' room. Our bedrooms may only have been separated by a narrow hallway, but each day we became more and more different. We were loyal to the choices we had made, or thought we had made, with the result that neither of us could avoid being embarrassed, increasingly so, by what the other was becoming. With no problem at all, with no sense of separation at all, he fit in with the world around us, with the jobs that were available to us, with the future that was laid out for us. It would not be long before I was experiencing, and even cultivating, the feeling of an immense disjunction in my life, one both my studies and my homosexuality were working to create: I was not going to be a worker, not going to be a butcher, but rather something different from what I had been socially destined to become. He would perform his military service and get married immediately afterwards (he must have been 21 or 22), quickly having two children. As for me, I would begin university studies at the age of 18, would move out of my parents' house at the age of 20 (shortly after he did, in fact) in order to live alone and without interference. And I desperately wanted to be declared unfit for military service. (That is, in fact, what happened in the end, a few years later. After having received the maximum deferment that was permitted for students, I pretended to suffer from impaired vision and hearing during the "three days" that led up to being inducted. The result was that the doctor in charge of the barracks at Vincennes asked me: "What is your occupation?" "I am preparing for the *agrégation* in Philosophy." "I think it would be better for all concerned if you continued with that, then." I was 25 years old at the time, and it was all I could do to control the jubilation I felt at that moment enough to keep it hidden.)

4

I WENT NEARLY THIRTY-FIVE YEARS without seeing this brother of mine with whom I spent my childhood and a good part of my adolescence. At the time I write these pages, he lives off of disability benefits in Belgium, because he is today physically incapable of performing what his work (or any form of work) requires of him: carrying animal carcasses around year after year has destroyed his shoulders. And if I no longer have any connection with him, it is, as I already pointed out, entirely my fault.

We were already like strangers to each other while we were still living together. Then, in the two or three years after we had both moved out, when we would see each other at family gatherings, the tie between us was only that we had a past in common and that we each had a relationship with our parents, his a close one, and mine distant.

I watched his satisfaction with everything I wanted to leave behind, his enjoyment of all those things I detested. To depict my feelings for him, I could cite nearly word for word what John Edgar Wideman wrote about his brother in *Brothers and Keepers*: "One measure of my success was the distance I'd put between us." It couldn't be better said. In a certain way, this means that my brother implicitly served as a reference point for me. What I wanted could be summed up like this: not to be like him. Talking to his brother in his mind, Wideman poses the question: "Was I as much a stranger to you as you seemed to me?" Did I ask myself this question all those years ago? I knew the answer, and it in fact made me happy, since I was trying in every way I could think of to become different from him. I recognized myself again in something else Wideman wrote: "Because we were brothers, holidays, family celebrations, and troubles drew us to the same rooms at the same time, but I felt uncomfortable around you."[11] In fact, in my case, everything about these occasions made me uncomfortable, since my brother fitted well into the world that was already no longer mine, except that it really still was. To the extent that for Wideman, "running away from Pittsburgh, from poverty, from blackness" and attending university represented a path of voluntary exile, it seems obvious how difficult it would have been for him to retrace his steps at regular intervals. Each time he returned home, he couldn't help but find there, unchanged, the same reality that had made him want to leave— a discovery that allowed him to notice with the passage of time his increasing success at distancing himself. This would not stop him from feeling guilty faced with those he left behind. But it was a guilt accompanied by fear: "Fear marched along beside guilt. Fear of acknowledging in myself any traces of the poverty, ignorance, and danger I'd find surrounding me when I returned to Pittsburgh." Yes, a fear that "I was contaminated and would carry the poison wherever I ran. Fear that the evil would be discovered in me and I'd be shunned like a leper." The observation he arrives at in thinking about his brother is in the end quite simple: "Your world. The blackness that incriminated me."[12] I could use the same words, the same phrases, as regards my way of perceiving my brother at the time: your world, working class culture, the "culture of the poor" that was like an accusation directed at me, one that I was afraid would stick to my skin even in my headlong flight from it. I needed to exorcise the devil in me, to get it out—or else to make it invisible, so that no one could detect its presence. For many years this was something I worked on during every moment of my life.

Citing these few lines from Wideman allows me to give a description of the burden I carried with me everywhere during my adolescence, and for many years after. It was as if his words spoke of me (even if I am perfectly aware, should it need saying, that this transposition has its limits. If I can recognize myself in the description Wideman gives of the disintegration of his connections to his family, and especially to his brother, or, more precisely, the transformation of these connections into relations of distance and rejection, obviously the situation he describes is quite different from mine. For he came from a poor, black neighborhood in Pittsburgh, and went on to become a professor and a famous writer while his brother was sentenced to life in prison for murder. This is the tragic history that he is trying to understand in his magnificent book.)

Wideman is right to insist on the fact that he had to make a choice, and he made one. I, too, had to choose. Like him, I chose myself. But the sense of guilt that he describes is one I felt only intermittently. The sense of my own freedom was intoxicating, as was the joy of escaping from what had been my destiny. All this left little room for remorse. I really have no idea what my brother must think about all of this these days, what he might say when he talks about the subject—when, for instance, someone asks him if we are related after one of my appearances (which I try to keep infrequent) on television.

Imagine my surprise upon learning from my mother that my two younger brothers (eight and fourteen years younger than me) felt that I had "abandoned" them, and had been very hurt by this abandonment! At least one of them still feels hurt by it. I had never really asked myself how they must have perceived my increasing and then total estrangement. What were their feelings? How did they think of me? What was I to them? It was as if I became a ghost in their lives, one about whom they might later speak to their wives and children. But those wives and children would never meet me. When one of my younger brothers went through a divorce, his wife, who had never met me, hurled the following reproach at him amidst a series of other complaints (my mother told me this): "And your brother Didier is nothing but a faggot who abandoned his family." I can't really deny it. Didn't she give concise expression to a simple truth? To my truth?

I was selfish. I was out to save myself and didn't have the inclination—I was twenty years old!—to pay heed to any of the damage my flight might have caused. My two younger brothers followed more or less the same path through school as did my older brother. They enrolled in middle school (there was now only one track open for all students) at the age of eleven because they had to, and they left school as soon as it was allowed (at the age of 16), one of them having spent a few years vegetating in "vocational" classes in a technical high school and the other in a literary track. ("I wasn't cut out for school," one of them told me recently, replying to some questions I had sent him in an email as I was writing this book.) Neither of them continued on to the Baccalaureate exam. The older of the two wanted to become a mechanic. Today he sells cars on the island of Réunion. My mother tells me he makes a good living. The second joined the army at the age of 17, and he has stayed in the military. Or, more precisely, he joined the police force and has risen a bit in the ranks. Both of them vote for the right, of course, having been until quite recently loyal supporters of the National Front. This means that when I joined demonstrations protesting the electoral successes of the extreme right, or when I showed my support for immigrants and undocumented workers, I was demonstrating against my own family! But I could also put things the other way round and say that it was my family that rose up against everything that I supported and thus against everything that I was, everything I represented in their eyes (a Parisian intellectual totally out of touch with reality, understanding nothing of the problems of the working class). Still, the fact that my brothers voted for a political party that horrifies me, and then for a presidential candidate who belonged to a more classic version of the right wing party but understood how to appeal to this part of the electorate, seems to be so much the result of a kind of sociological necessity, seems so clearly to follow certain social laws (as, indeed, do my political choices), that I am left feeling a bit baffled. It is no longer as clear to me as it used to be how I should react to all of this. It seems easy to convince yourself in the abstract that you will never speak to anyone who votes for the National Front, never shake their hand. But how do you react when you discover that these people are part of your own family? What do you say? What do you do? What do you think?

We can see that my two younger brothers both managed to rise above the situation that my parents had lived in, so we could speak here of upward social mobility, even if it still remains basically within the space of the class of origin, limited in its extent by that class and the determinisms associated with it, notably the voluntary choice to leave school which immediately restricts the kinds of jobs or professional careers open to anyone who has been excluded from the educational system and led to believe that they chose that very exclusion.

Now I have to face a certain set of questions: What if I had taken an interest in them? What if I had helped them with their studies? What if I had tried to teach them a love of reading? After all, that one should study, that reading is enjoyable, that books are something you can love—these are not universally distributed attitudes, but are in fact closely correlated with social conditions and with the background you come from. These very social conditions led my younger brothers, like almost everyone else around them, to refuse and to reject that towards which some miracle had managed to move me. Should I have realized that such a miracle could in fact happen over again? That it might even be less improbable a recurrence once it had already happened to one of us (to me!), since that first lucky person would then be able to transmit not only what he had learned, but also the desire to learn, to those coming after him. But this would have required time and patience; it would have required that I remain in close contact with my family. Would that have been enough to overcome the implacable logic of academic tracking? Would it have enabled us to push back against the mechanisms of social reproduction whose efficacy is produced in large part by the inertia of a class *habitus*? There was no way in which I served as the "guardian" of my brothers, with the result that it is now difficult for me—knowing that it is rather late for this feeling—not to feel guilty.

Well before I ever experienced these feelings of "guilt," I saw myself and thought of myself as a "miracle case" within the educational system. That is to say, it became clear to me quite early on that the destinies of my three brothers were not or would not be identical to or analogous with mine, by which I mean that the effect of the social verdict that had been delivered in each of our cases even before we were born would strike each of them with much greater violence than would happen to me. In another of his novels, titled *Fanon*, Wideman gives a compelling description of the power of verdicts like these, and the awareness he has always had of this phenomenon—along with the feeling that he has always had of being another miraculous exception—escaping, as he did, from the different destinies that might have been his. His brother is in prison. He goes to visit him with his mother. He knows it could have been him behind bars, and asks himself why it isn't him and how he managed to escape from what seems like an inevitability for young black men from underprivileged neighborhoods: "How many black men in prison for how long, you could get confused by numbers, staggeringly large numbers, outraged by dire probabilities and obvious disproportions. Ugly masses of brute statistics impossible to make sense of, but some days a single possibility's enough to overwhelm me—how likely, how easy, after all, it would be to be my brother. Our fortunes exchanged, his portion mine, mine his. I recall all those meals at the same table, sleeping for years under the same roof, sharing the same parents and siblings (almost), same grandparents uncles aunts nieces cousins nephews, the point being, the point the numbers reveal: it would be a less than startling outcome to find myself incarcerated."[13] Wideman forces us to admit the following: the irrefutable fact that certain people—doubtless a good number of people—deviate from "statistics" or elude the implacable logic of "numbers" in no way nullifies the sociological truth of those statistics and those numbers. This is true no matter what the advocates of the ideology of "personal merit" would have us believe. Had I followed the same path as my brothers, would I be like them? That is, would I have voted for the National Front? Would I wax indignant about the "foreigners" who are invading our land and acting "as if they belong here"? Would I share with them the same kinds of reactions to and the same defensive discourse about what they consider to be the aggressive actions they suffer from at the hands of society, the State, the "elite," the "powerful," or "others" more generally? To which "us" would I belong? To which "them" would I be opposed? In short, what would be my politics? What would be my way either of resisting the order of things or else adhering to it?

Wideman has no hesitation in speaking about a war against black people. (And he is obviously not the first person to look at American society in this way. There is a long tradition of thought—and of experience—behind such a point of view.) He says as much to his mother: "There's a war going on, a war being waged against people like us all over the world and this prison visiting room one of the battlefields." His mother replies that he is exaggerating, that she sees things differently and prefers to emphasize individual responsibility in the way all these dramas unfold. Still he defends his position: "a war waged by an enemy most of us don't think of as an enemy, a total war waged by an implacable foe."[14] This is the idea that is played out in the novel, in which he weaves together political reflection on a racially divided America and a meditation on Frantz Fanon and on the importance of Fanon's life and work for black consciousness, self-affirmation, pride, for a politics of the self, or, quite simply, for "black anger," and thus for resistance in the face of the enemy in all its omnipotence and omnipresence. Then there is the fact that his brother, long before he was arrested, during his adolescence, kept a copy of *Black Skins, White Masks* in his pocket, promising himself he would read it one day. How important a book can be for someone before they've even read it! It can be enough just to know that it was important for other people you feel close to.

Is it possible to take the transposition I suggested earlier even a little further and to speak of an implacable war society prosecutes, in its most banal activities and its most ordinary operations, a war led by the bourgeoisie, by the dominant classes, by an invisible enemy—or all too visible—, against the working classes in general? It would be enough to take a look at the statistics concerning prison populations in France or in Europe to be convinced: the "numbers" would speak elegantly of the "dire probability" that young men from destitute suburbs—especially those who are labeled "children of immigrants"—will end up behind bars. And it doesn't seem at all exaggerated to describe the suburban housing projects, the "*cités*," that surround French cities as constituting today the theatre of a latent civil war: the situation in these urban ghettos provides clear evidence of the ways certain categories of the population are treated, how they are pushed to the margins of social and political life, reduced to poverty, to a precarious existence, deprived of a future. The huge revolts that flare up at regular intervals in these "neighborhoods" are simply the sudden condensation of a multitude of fragmentary battles whose rumbling never entirely goes away.

But I would also be tempted to add that there is really no other interpretation possible of other statistical realities such as the systematic elimination of the working class from the educational system and the situations of segregation and of social inferiority to which such mechanisms condemn them. I know people will accuse me of falling into the realm of conspiracy theories, ascribing hidden purposes to certain institutions and even inventing evil intentions. This is the same criticism Bourdieu offered of the Althusserian notion of "ideological state apparatuses." Such a notion involves thinking in terms of a "pessimistic functionalism." An apparatus, he writes, would be "an infernal machine, programmed to accomplish certain purposes," adding that "this fantasy of the conspiracy, the idea that an evil will is responsible for everything that happens in the social world, haunts critical social thought."[15] Of course he is right! It is undeniable that Althusser's concept returns us to an old fashioned Marxist dramaturgy—or better, an old fashioned Marxist logomachy—in which entities written with capital letters confront each other as if on a stage in some theatre (in a purely scholastic kind of way). Still, it is worth pointing out that certain formulations by Bourdieu are surprisingly close to what he seems so insistent here on dismissing, even if, in his case, it is less a matter of revealing a hidden will and more about pointing out "objective results." An example is when he writes: "What is the real function of an educational system when it functions in such a way that across the entire educational spectrum children from the working classes and, to a lesser extent, from the middle classes, find themselves eliminated from the system?"[16]

The "real function"! Obvious and undeniable. So, like Wideman, who refuses to give up his immediate perception of the world in spite of the reasonable observations his mother makes, I cannot help but see an infernal machine in the school system, given the way it functions right in front of our eyes. If it is not set up to attain this goal, it at least produces this objective result: rejecting the children of the working class, perpetuating and legitimating class domination, differential access to careers and to social positions. A war is going on against the underdogs and schools are one of the battlefields. Teachers do the best they can! But in fact there is little or nothing they can do when faced with the irresistible forces of the social order, forces that operate both in secret and in the light of day, and that impose themselves everywhere and on everyone.

1

I MENTIONED EARLIER that during my childhood my entire family was "communist," in the sense that the Communist Party was the organizing principle and the uncontested horizon of our relation to politics. How could my family have turned into one in which it seemed possible, even natural sometimes, to vote either for the right or for the extreme right?

What had happened to create a situation in which so many people whose spontaneous reactions had been ones of visceral disgust when they came across figures they took to be enemies of the working class, people who had happily hurled abuse at the television when such figures appeared on the screen (a strange but effective way of taking comfort in one's beliefs and one's sense of self), would begin voting for the National Front? I am sure this is what transpired in my father's case. And what had happened to produce a situation in which a good number of these people, having voted for the National Front in the first round of elections would, in the second round, cast their vote for the candidate of the traditional right wing, someone they would have treated with contempt in an earlier moment? (This finally led to a situation in which even in the first round of the election they voted for a caricatural representative of the bourgeois business classes, who, thanks to their votes, was elected President of the

Republic.) What heavy measure of responsibility for this process must be borne by the official left wing? What is the responsibility of those people who, having set aside the political commitments they held in the 1960s and 1970s as the youthful follies of a bygone moment, having risen to positions of power and importance, would do all they could to encourage the spread of right wing thinking, would consign to the dustbin of history anything associated with what had once been one of the essential preoccupations of the left (even, since the middle of the nineteenth century, one of its fundamental characteristics), which is to say the attention paid to oppression, to social conflict, or simply to the effort to create a space within the political sphere for the oppressed? It was not just the "worker's movement" with its traditions and its struggles that disappeared from political and intellectual discourse and from the public stage. Gone, as well, were the workers themselves, their culture, the conditions under which they lived, their aspirations...[1]

When I was a young leftist (Trotskyist) in high school, my father was constantly ranting about "students" who were "always trying to tell us what to do" and who "in ten years will be coming back and giving us orders." His reaction, as intransigent as it was visceral, seemed to me then to be contrary to the "historical interests of the working class" and to be the result of the influence wielded over that class by an outdated Communist Party that had never fully left the Stalinist moment behind and was doing all it could to prevent the arrival of an inevitable revolution. But nowadays how is it possible to think that my father was wrong? Look at what has become of all those who back then had been advocating civil war, intoxicated by the mythology of the proletarian revolution! These days they are just as sure of themselves as ever, just as vehement, but, with only one or two exceptions, their vehemence is focused on opposing the slightest hint of protest arising from the working classes. They have returned to what had originally been promised to them—they have become what they were destined to be—and in doing so they have turned themselves into the enemies of all those people whose vanguard they used to claim to represent, people they accused of being too timid and too corrupted by middle-class aspirations. It is said that one day in May 1968, Marcel Jouhandeau, seeing a column of student protestors passing by, sneered at them: "Go back home! In twenty years, you'll all be bankers." We could say he was of more or less the same opinion as my father, even if his reasons for arriving at that opinion were the exact opposite. And, of course, he was right. Maybe not bankers, but "important" people without a doubt, people whose astonishing career paths established them, whether politically, intellectually, or personally, in comfortable positions in the social order, turning them into the defenders of things as they are, the defenders of a world perfectly suited to the people they had become.

In 1981, when François Mitterrand made it possible to hope for a victory for the left, he managed to win over a quarter of Communist Party voters. The Communist Party's own candidate only received 15% of the votes in the first round, compared to 20 or 21% in the legislative elections of 1977. This erosion of support, a prelude to the total collapse that would soon take place, can be explained to a great extent by the inability of the "Party of the Working Class" to evolve and to break from the

Soviet regime (which provided, it is true, a good deal of its financial support). But it was also due to its inability to take seriously the new social movements that developed in the wake of May 1968. To put it mildly, the Party no longer seemed to have much of a relation to the forms of desire for social transformation and for political innovation that characterized the 1960s and 1970s, and that in some ways realized themselves in 1981. And yet the victory of the left, along with the government it put into place (which would include some communists) soon produced a strong sense of disillusionment in working class circles, and a loss of interest in the politicians whom they had previously trusted, and for whom they had voted. Soon they felt betrayed and neglected by them. I remember often hearing the observation (my mother repeated it to me every time we spoke): "Right or left, there's no difference; they are all the same, and the same people always end up footing the bill."

The socialist left set out on a major project of transformation, one that became more and more marked as the years went by. With a suspicious degree of enthusiasm, they started to turn to neoconservative intellectuals for guidance. Those intellectuals, pretending to offer a way to renovate leftist thought, in fact set out to eliminate all that was leftist from the left. What actually occurred was a general and quite thoroughgoing metamorphosis of the *ethos* of the party as well as of its intellectual references. Gone was any talk of exploitation and resistance, replaced by talk of "necessary modernization" and of "radical social reform"; gone the references to relations between the classes, replaced by talk of a "life in common"; gone any mention of unequal social opportunities, replaced by an emphasis on "individual responsibility." The notion of domination, and the very idea of a structuring opposition between those in positions of dominance and those who were dominated disappeared from the official political landscape on the left, replaced by a more neutral idea of a "social contract" or a "social compact," providing a framework within which individuals who were defined as "having equal rights" ("Equal?" What an obscene idea!) were encouraged to set aside their "particular interests" (that is, they should keep their mouths shut and let the government do its job). What were the ideological objectives of this so-called "political philosophy," one that spread widely and was celebrated throughout the media as well as the political and intellectual fields on both the right and on the left? (Its promoters in fact did their best to eliminate any frontier between the right and the left, while encouraging the left—a willing partner—to move ever rightward.) The stakes were hardly hidden: the extolling of the virtues of the "autonomous subject," and the accompanying effort to do away with any form of thought that took into account historical and social forms of determinism were mainly intended to dismiss the idea that specific social groups—"classes"—existed, and so to justify dismantling the welfare state and other forms of social protection. This was done in the name of a necessary individualization (or decollectivization, or desocialization) of the right to work and of systems of solidarity and of redistribution. Up until this moment such age-old discourses and projects had always been a hallmark of the right; it would obsessively trot them out, lauding individual responsibility as opposed to "collectivism." Now they became the discourses and projects of a good part of the left. The situation could basically be summed up like this: The parties of the left, along with party intellectuals and state intellectuals, began from this moment forward to think and speak the language of those who govern, no longer the language of those who are governed. They spoke in the name of the government (and as part of it), no longer in the name of the governed (and as part of them). And so of course they adopted a governing point of view on the world, disdainfully dismissing (and doing so with great discursive violence, a violence that was experienced as such by those at whom it was directed) the point of view of those being governed. The most that any of them would deign to do (in the Christian and philanthropic versions of these neoconservative discourses) would be to replace the oppressed and dominated of yesterday—along with their struggles—with the "marginalized" of today—who were presumed to be of a passive nature. They could be considered as the silent potential recipients of the benefits of various technocratic measures that were intended to help the "poor" and the "victims" of "precarity" and of "disaffiliation." All this was nothing other than a hypocritical and underhanded strategy meant to invalidate any approach to these problems that used terms such as oppression and struggle, or reproduction or transformation of social structures, or inertia and dynamism within class antagonisms.[2]

This shift in political discourse transformed the way the social world could be perceived, and therefore, in a performative manner, it transformed the social world itself, given that that world is produced by the very categories of thought by means of which it is perceived. But making political discourse about "classes" and class relations disappear, eliminating classes and class relations as cognitive and theoretical categories, does nothing to prevent those people who live under the objective conditions that the word "class" was used to designate from feeling abandoned by those people now preaching to them about the wonders of the "social compact," and simultaneously about how urgent and "necessary" it was to deregulate the economy and to dismantle the welfare state.[3] Whole sectors of the most severely disadvantaged would thus, in what almost seemed like an automatic reshuffling of the cards in the political deck, shift over to the only party that seemed to care about them, the only one, in any case, that offered them a discourse that seemed intended to provide meaning to the experiences that made up their daily lives. This happened despite the fact that the leadership of that party was not made up of people from the working class—far from it! Things had been different in the case of the Communist Party, which was always careful to choose activists from the working class itself, so that voters could identify with them. My mother did finally admit to me, after having denied it for a very long time, that she had voted for the National Front. ("But only once," she insisted, even though I am not sure I believe her on this point. "It was in order to make a point, because things weren't going right," she offered as a justification once the unpleasantness of the confession was behind her. Then, strangely, she added, regarding the decision to vote for Le Pen in the first round of the elections, "The people who voted for him didn't really want to see him elected. In the second round we all voted normally.")[4]

Unlike voting communist, a way of voting that could be assumed forthrightly and asserted publicly, voting for the extreme right seems to have been something that needed to be kept secret, even denied in the face of some "outside" instance of judgment (which is what I appear to have represented, in my family's eyes). Such a vote had nonetheless been carefully thought over and decided upon. The former way of voting was a proud affirmation of one's class identity, a political gesture confirming that very identity by offering support to the "workers' party." The latter kind of vote was a silent act in defense of whatever was left of such an identity, to which the ruling powers of the institutionalized left paid no attention, or else treated dismissively. They had all graduated from the École Nationale d'Administration or other bourgeois institutions whose function was to produce technocrats. Such places produce and inculcate a "dominant ideology" that has become generalized across all political divisions. (One cannot insist too much on the extent to which elite circles of the "modernist"—and often Christian—left contributed to the development of this rightist dominant ideology. It is hardly surprising that a former socialist party leader—from the north of France, of course, and thus coming from a different class background and a different political culture—felt it to be his heartfelt duty to remind his friends during the presidential election campaign of 2002 that "worker" was not a dirty word.) However paradoxical it might seem to some people, I am convinced that voting for the National Front must be interpreted, at least in part, as the final recourse of people of the working classes attempting to defend their collective identity, or to defend, in any case, a dignity that was being trampled on—now even by those who had once been their representatives and defenders. Dignity is a fragile feeling, unsure of itself; it requires recognition and reassurances. People first of all have a need not to feel like they are being treated as a negligible quantity, or merely as an entry in a statistical table or on a balance sheet, which is to say mute objects about which political decisions are made. If a time comes when those in whom you have placed your confidence seem no longer to deserve it, you place your confidence in others. Even if it happens bit by bit, you end up turning to new representatives.[5]

So whose fault is it that the new representatives people turn to are of a certain ilk? Whose fault if the meaning of a "we" sustained or reconstituted in this way undergoes a transformation such that it comes to mean the "French" as opposed to "foreigners," whereas it had used to mean "workers" as opposed to the "bourgeoisie"? Or, to put it more precisely, whose fault is it if the opposition between "worker" and "bourgeois," even if it continues to exist in the form of an opposition between the "have nots" and the "haves" (which is not exactly the same opposition—it carries different political consequences), takes on a national and racial dimension, with the "haves" being perceived as favorably inclined to immigration and the "have nots" as suffering on a daily basis because of this same immigration, one that is held to be responsible for all their difficulties?

The claim could be made that voting communist represented a positive form of self-affirmation, whereas voting for the National Front represented a negative one. (In the first case, the links to party structures, to party spokespersons, to the coherence of the political discourse in question and its correspondence to a certain class identity, were all quite strong and conclusive; but in the second case such links were nearly inexistent or else quite secondary.) Yet in both cases the outcome of the voting was meant to be, or became in fact, the public manifestation of a group that was giving itself an organization by means of votes cast individually, but also collectively, in order to make its voice heard. What organized itself around the Communist Party was the collective vote of a group conscious of itself and anchored both in the objective conditions of its existence and in a political tradition. Other categories would affiliate with this group when their perception of the world and their political agenda would align, in either the short or the long term, with those of the "working class" in its manifestation as a class-subject. By erasing any idea of social groups with conflicting relations to each other from leftist political discourse (indeed by going so far as to replace the structuring affirmation of a conflictual society, in which one's obligation was to support the demands of the working class, with a denunciation of social movements that were claimed to be relics of the past, that were, along with their supporters, taken to be somehow archaic, or some kind of a sign of the deterioration of the social bond that the government's project should be to restore), the goal was to succeed at depriving people who voted together of the possibility of thinking of themselves as a group held together by common interests and shared preoccupations. Their opinions were reduced to individual ones, and those opinions were dissociated from any of the power they might have held in the past, doomed henceforth to a kind of powerlessness. But that powerlessness turned into anger. The result was inevitable: the group reformed, but in a different way, and the class that had been deconstructed by the neoconservative discourses of the left found a new way to organize itself and to make its point of view known.

One sees here the limits of the wonderful analysis Sartre gives of electoral systems and of election seasons as processes of individualization and therefore of the depoliticization of opinion—a "serial" kind of situation—, as opposed to the collective and politicizing formation of thought that happens in the course of a movement or a period of political mobilization—a "group" situation.[6] It is certainly true that his example is striking: the workers who participated in the major strikes of May 1968 but then only a month later saved the Gaullist regime by voting for its candidates. Yet this example shouldn't cause us to forget that the act of voting, while fundamentally individual in appearance, can be experienced as part of a collective mobilization, as a political action carried out in common with others. Viewed in this way, it contravenes the very principle of the system of "universal suffrage," in which the aggregation of individual voices is meant to produce the expression of the "general will" that in theory transcends any particular desires. But in the situation I have just described (voting communist or voting for the National Front), the opposite happens: a class war is carried out at the ballot box, a practice of confrontation is reproduced election after election, in which one class—or a part of one class—is seen doing its best to make its presence manifest in the face of others, to set up a power relation. Merleau-Ponty, too, while emphasizing that "the vote consults people at rest, outside their job, outside their life," that is, according to an abstract and individualizing logic, insists on the fact that "when we vote, it is a form of violence": "Each rejects the suffrage of the others."[7] Far from seeking to collaborate in defining all together what the "general will" of the people might be, far from contributing to the establishment of a consensus or to the emergence of a majority to whose wishes a minority would agree to acquiesce, the working class, or some part of it (and in this it is like any other class: think of the reaction of the bourgeoisie each time the left is elected to power), is there ready to contest the claim that some elected majority represents the "general" point of view by recalling that it considers this majority's point of view to be that of an adversary who is defending its own interests in opposition to one's own. As far as the vote for the National Front is concerned, this process by which a political self is constructed happened through an alliance—at least while the electoral campaign was underway—with social strata that at other times would have been considered to be made up of "enemies." The major effect of the disappearance of the "working class" and of workers—or even, we might say, of the popular classes more generally—from political discourse will thus have been the weakening of the long-standing alliances formed under the banner of "the left" between the working-class world and certain other social categories (workers in the public sector, teachers, and so on), and the formation of a new "historical bloc," to use Gramsci's vocabulary, bringing together large portions of the vulnerable popular classes living under conditions of precarity with shopkeepers and tradespeople, or with well-to-do retirees in the south of France, or even with fascist military types or traditional old Catholic families, and thus largely located on the right or even the far right.[8] But this was doubtless what was required at a given moment in order to have any political weight—all the more so since that weight had to be thrown against the left that was in power or, more exactly, against the power that the parties of the left incarnated. Indeed, this gesture was perceived as the only way to go on living. Yet obviously, with the formation of new alliances and new political configurations, this group—which included only a part of the former group organized around voting communist—became different from what it had been. Those who made it up began thinking of themselves, of their political interests and of their relations to political and social lives in completely different ways.

Voting for the National Front was probably not, for most of these voters, the same kind of thing that voting for the Communist Party had been: this new vote was more intermittent and less consistent. It was not with the same solidarity or the same intensity that people gave themselves or their thoughts over to the spokespersons who would represent them on the political stage. By means of their vote for the Communist Party, individuals went beyond what they were separately or serially, and the collective opinion that was produced through the mediation of the Party, which both shaped and expressed it, was in no way the reflection of the various heterogeneous opinions of any of the voters; but in voting for the National Front, individuals remain individuals and the opinion they produce is simply the sum of their spontaneous prejudices, latched onto by the party, and taken up and formulated into a coherent political program. Yet even if those people who vote for the party do not subscribe to the entirety of its program, the strength gained by the party in this way allows it to believe that its voters are in agreement with its whole discourse.

It is tempting to say that what we have in this case is a serial collective, one deeply marked by seriality—given that what predominates here are impulsive reactions, opinions that may be shared but are more received ones than they are interests thought out collectively or opinions arrived at through practical forms of action. It is a kind of alienated vision (leveling accusations at foreigners) rather than a politicized concept (a struggle against domination). Nonetheless, this "collective" becomes a "group" by means of its vote for a party which can then, with the consent of those voters, instrumentalize the very means of expression chosen and used by those who themselves instrumentalized that party in order to make their voices heard.[9]

We should in any case remark that to a large degree voting for someone rarely amounts to more than a partial or oblique adherence to the discourse or platforms of the party or the candidate in question—and this is true for all voters. When I observed to my mother that by voting for Le Pen she had supported a party that actively opposed abortion rights, whereas I knew she had had an abortion, she replied: "But that's got nothing to do with it. That's not why I voted for him." If that is the case, then how does someone choose the elements that count, that weigh in favor of a decision to vote for a candidate, and the elements that are deliberately set aside? Surely the essential factor is the feeling of knowing or believing that you are being both individually and collectively represented, even if it is in an incomplete and imperfect kind of way. That is, what counts is that one feels supported by those one supports; one has the impression of existing and of counting for something in the life of politics by means of participating in an election, by means of a decision to act in this way.

These two antagonistic political visions (the one embodied in a vote for the Communist Party, and the one embodied in a vote for the National Front), these two modes of constituting oneself as a political subject relied on different categories for perceiving and dividing up the social world. (These divergent categories of perception could certainly co-exist in a single individual, caught up in different temporalities of course, but also tied to different places, related to different structures of daily life in which that individual may be involved: it might depend on whether the accent is placed on the practical solidarity that functions within the confines of the factory or the feeling of competition involved in holding on to one's job, or whether the accent is placed on the feeling of belonging to an informal network of parents who pick up their children from the same school or on a feeling of exasperation at how difficult life in the neighborhood is becoming, and so on.) They are opposite, or at least divergent, ways of dividing up social reality and of trying to exercise some influence on the political orientation of those in the government, but the two ways are not mutually exclusive. That is why, however long-lasting and however disconcerting the alliances that went into forming the National Front electorate may be, it is not at all impossible, and even less is it unthinkable, that some of those people—and only some of them—might be found in a more or less near future voting for the extreme left. This is not to say that the extreme left and the extreme right should be placed on the same level—as is often done by those people who are trying to protect their monopoly over what can be said to constitute legitimate politics. (They make this claim by systematically accusing any point of view, any act of self-affirmation that doesn't correspond to their definition of politics of being "populist." Such accusations merely reveal their lack of understanding—which is class-based—of what they take to be the "irrationality" of the people whenever they do not simply agree to submit to the "reason" and "wisdom" of those in power.) But it is to say that the political mobilization of a group—the world of workers and of the popular classes—by means of electoral politics can shift its location radically on the political chessboard; if the overall situation (national and international) shifts, such a mobilization could crystallize within the framework of a different "historical bloc" involving other segments of society. Yet doubtless a certain number of significant events have to take place—strikes, protests, and so on—for any such transformation to come about. It is not all that easy to undo a mental sense of political belonging that is of long duration—even when that sense has been unstable and uncertain—, just as it is not possible to create in a single day a new way of relating to oneself and to others, a new way of looking at the world, a different discourse on the way life works.

2

I AM, OF COURSE, aware of the fact that both the discourse and the success of the National Front were in many ways encouraged by, and even seemed an answer to, feelings that had a lively presence in the popular classes in the 1960s and 1970s. If someone had wanted to deduce a political program from the kinds of remarks that were made on a daily basis in my family during those years, at a time when everyone was still voting on the left, the result would not have been very different from the future electoral platforms of this far right party in the 1980s and 1990s: a desire to deport immigrants and to set up a system of "national preferences" for employment and for social services, support for an increasingly repressive penal system, for the idea of capital punishment and the widespread application of it, support for the right to leave school at age 14, and so on. The extreme right's ability to attract those who had previously voted communist (or to appeal to younger voters who started out voting for the National Front, since it seems that children of workers voted for the extreme right both more easily and more systematically than did their elders[10]) was made possible or at least facilitated by the profound racism that constituted one of the dominant characteristics of white working and lower class circles. Remarks that would flourish everywhere and be directed at Maghrebi families in the 1980s —"It's an invasion; they are taking over;" "They're getting all the welfare payments, and leaving nothing for us," and so on, *ad nauseum*—had been preceded for at least thirty years by radically hostile ways of perceiving workers who came from the Maghreb, of speaking with them, and of behaving towards them.[11] This hostility was already visible both during the Algerian War ("If they want their independence so badly, why can't they just stay at home?"), and after Algeria had won its independence ("They wanted their independence. Now that they have it, it's time they went home."). But it became even worse throughout the 1960s and 1970s. The scorn that the French felt for them would be apparent notably in the way they were systematically addressed with the pronoun *tu* instead of *vous*. When people talked about them, the only words used were *bicots*, *ratons*, or other highly insulting terms. In those years, "immigrants" were mostly single men who lived in hostels and insalubrious hotels, where "sleep merchants" increased their profits by inflicting degrading living conditions on them. That would all change with the massive arrival of a new generation of immigrants, and also with the establishment of families and the birth of children: an entire population of people with origins outside France would move into the large low income housing projects that had only recently been built, and that had until then only been lived in by French people or by immigrants from other European countries. When, in the mid 1960s, my parents obtained an apartment in one of those housing projects on the edge of town, where I would live between the ages of 13 and 20, only white people lived in the building. It was towards the end of the 1970s—I had been gone for a long while—that Maghrebi families moved in, rapidly becoming the largest group in the neighborhood. These changes caused a dramatic exacerbation of the racist impulses that had always been present in everyday conversations. Yet it was as if what was happening was the creation of two different levels of consciousness that only rarely came into contact, since this new situation didn't seem to interfere immediately with the reasoned political choices people were making, be it choosing to vote for a political party—"the Party"—that had actively opposed the war in Algeria, or becoming a member of a union—the CGT—that was at least officially opposed to racism, or, more generally, maintaining one's perception of oneself as a leftist member of the working class.

In fact, when people voted for the left, in a certain way they voted against certain kinds of unthinking impulses, and thus against a part of themselves. The racist feelings in question were certainly strong ones and, in fact, the Communist Party was not above encouraging them in quite odious ways on a number of occasions. But they never became established as the kernel of a set of political preoccupations. Sometimes, in fact, people felt obliged to apologize for such remarks when they made them to a circle that was larger than that of the immediate family. In such circumstances, it was not at all unusual to hear sentences that began "I've never been racist, but…," or that ended, "Not that I'm racist, of course." Or else someone would intersperse the conversation with remarks such as, "They are like any group; they aren't all bad," and then someone would mention the example of this or that "buddy" at the factory as a fellow who had done this or that. And so on. It took time for the daily expressions of ordinary racism to join up with more directly ideological elements and become transformed into a hegemonic way of perceiving the social world. This was something that happened under the effect of a discourse that was organized in such a way so as to encourage such forms of expression and give them meaning on a public stage.

It was because my parents couldn't bear the new environment that had become predominant in their old neighborhood any longer that they decided to move out of their apartment there and into a housing development in Muizon. They were running away from what seemed to them to be a set of enormous new threats that had erupted into a world that had once been theirs, and that they felt was being taken away from them. My mother began complaining about the "swarms" of children belonging to the new arrivals who urinated and defecated in the stairways and who, once they were teenagers, transformed the housing complex into a world of delinquency, producing a climate of fear and insecurity. She was indignant about the way the building was becoming run down—the walls of the stairways, the doors to the basement storage rooms, the mailboxes in the entryway would no sooner be repaired than they'd be damaged or defaced again; people's mail and newspapers were stolen regularly. This is not to mention all the damage done to cars parked in the streets: side mirrors broken, paintwork scratched, and so on. She could no longer bear the incessant noise and the smells of a kind of cooking that was unfamiliar to her, nor the cries of the sheep that was butchered in the bathroom of the apartment above hers to celebrate *Eid al-Kabir*. Did her descriptions really correspond to the reality around her or only to her fantasies? Most likely both at once. I no longer lived with them and never visited them, so I have no way of judging. When I would say to her on the telephone—for she would talk about almost nothing else—that she must be exaggerating, she would reply: "It's obvious that you don't live here and that it's not like that where you live." What could I say? Still, I ask myself about how certain discourses come into being, discourses that serve to transform problems of how to get along with your neighbors—and no doubt these are weighty problems—into a way of conceiving of the world, into a system of political thought. What histories are such discourses tied to? From what social depths do they arise? Based on what new modalities for constituting political subjectivities do they coagulate and take solid form as a vote for a party of the extreme right and for the kind of leader who had until then inspired only reactions of violent anger? Once such discourses had been ratified by and started reverberating within the mediatized space of politics, these spontaneous categories of perception, and the divisions they relied on ("French" people as opposed to "foreigners") began imposing themselves as somehow ever more "obvious." They were taken up more and more frequently in banal daily conversations within immediate families, within extended families, or while out shopping, or in the street, or at work, and so on. A crystallization of racist feeling was taking place in the social and political spaces that had previously been dominated by the Communist Party, and with it came a marked tendency to turn towards something on offer in the political world and claiming to be nothing other than an echo of the voice of the people and of a national feeling. In fact, it was this very political offering that had produced such sentiments in their present form by providing a coherent discursive framework and a social legitimacy to preexisting ill feelings and affects of resentment. The "common sense" that was shared by the "French" popular classes underwent a profound transformation, precisely because the quality of being "French" became its central element, replacing the quality of being a "worker," or a man or woman of the "left."

My family could stand as a representative case of the ordinary racism found in working class milieus in the 1960s and of the way it increased in harshness throughout the 1970s and 1980s. Members of my family were always employing a pejorative and insulting vocabulary (which my mother continues to use today) when speaking of the workers who came on their own from North Africa, and then of the families that either joined them or that were formed in France, and then of their children— children who are French because they were born in France, but are nonetheless perceived as being "immigrants," or in any case "foreigners." These insults could pop up at any moment, and at each occurrence they would be accentuated in such a way as to increase ten fold the acrimonious hostility they meant to express. *Crouillats* was one of the insults used, or *crouilles*, or *bougnoules* ... Because my complexion was quite dark, my mother would say to me regularly during my teenage years, "You look like a *crouille*." Or she would say, "From far off, you looked like a *bougnoule*." It is painfully obvious to me that the horror I felt in those years for my surroundings was linked to the consternation, or even the disgust that I felt faced with this kind of speech, something I encountered every day, and even many times each day. Just recently I invited my mother to spend a weekend in Paris. Her conversation was filled with this same vocabulary, something I rarely encounter, precisely because I have arranged my life so as not to have to deal with it: *bougnoules*, *négros*, *chinetoques*, and so on. When we were talking about the Barbès neighborhood where her mother had lived, a neighborhood that has for a long time been nearly exclusively one of people of African or Maghrebi origin, she asserted that she wouldn't want to live there, because "It's like another country where they live, it's not like home." I made a feeble attempt to argue with her, trying to hide my annoyance: "But Mom, Barbès is a neighborhood in Paris, it's part of our country." Her reply was simple: "You say whatever you like. I know what I mean." All I could do was mumble, "Well, I don't," meanwhile thinking to myself that this "return to Reims" that I had already begun writing about was proving to be no easy road, and that as a mental and social voyage, it might in the end be impossible to complete. Still, when I think back on it, I find myself asking whether my mother's racism, and the virulent scorn that she (the daughter of an immigrant!) always showed for immigrant workers in general and "Arabs" in particular, wasn't in some way a means for her—someone who had lived her life as part of a category that was always being reminded of its inferiority—to feel superior to people even more inferior than her. Was it a way of constructing a some-what valorized image of herself, something she accomplished through the devalorization of others; was it, in other words, simply a way of existing in her own eyes?

During the 1960s and 70s, the discourse of my parents, and especially that of my mother, mixed up two different ways of distinguishing between "us" and "them": there was a class distinction (between rich and poor) and an ethnic distinction (the "French" and "foreigners"). Different political circumstances could cause the accent to shift from one to the other of these distinctions. The great strikes of May 1968 brought together many different kinds of "workers," wherever they came from, united against their "bosses." One striking and successful slogan declared: "French workers, immigrant workers, same boss, same struggle." During more local, smaller scale strikes that followed, the same point of view prevailed. (The frontier was placed, in situations like these, between the strikers and "those on the side of the bosses," the "scabs.") Sartre was right to insist that before a strike the French worker is spontaneously racist and suspicious of immigrants, but once the strike is underway these bad feelings disappear and solidarity becomes predominant (even if it is partial or temporary). So it would seem that to a large extent it is the absence of political organization, or the absence of the perception that one belongs to an organized social group, that makes it possible for a racist form of division to replace a division based on class; it happens because of the absence of a sense of solidarity that comes from feeling the potential to participate in a political organization, a feeling that would mean that one is, in one's mind, continually politically engaged. At the point when the left has dissolved all such sense of political organization, one that had formed a horizon for people's self-perception, the group is then in a position to reconstitute itself around the other principle, a national one this time: the affirmation of oneself as the "legitimate" occupant of a territory of which one is feeling dispossessed or from which one feels one is being driven out. So the neighborhood you live in replaces the workplace and your position in a class hierarchy as part of your way of defining yourself and your way of relating to others. And more generally, your self affirmation depends on perceiving yourself as the natural master and owner of a country, as the sole legitimate beneficiary of the rights accorded by that country to its citizens. The very idea that "others" could profit from those rights—few though they may be—becomes unbearable, to the extent that it may seem that such a situation requires some kind of sharing that will result in a smaller portion being available for each of the interested parties. It is a form of self-affirmation that is activated in opposition to those to whom any legitimate form of belonging to the "Nation" is being denied, and to whom you would prefer to see refused all those rights you are attempting to hold onto for yourself at the very moment that the powers that be and the people who speak for those powers are calling them into question.

Yet we need to take this analysis even a step further if we wish to explain why at this or that moment the popular classes vote on the right. We need to ask if we are correct to assume, without questioning our assumption, that it is somehow more natural that those classes should vote on the left, especially given that it is not *always* the case that they do. And indeed it has never completely been the case that they do. After all, even when the Communist Party was doing well in electoral politics as the "party of the working class," only 30% of workers voted for it, and at least as many, if not more, voted for right-wing candidates than for all of the left-wing candidates together. And it is not simply elections that we are talking about here. Even popular or working class communal actions, marches or protests, can at different historical moments be anchored on the right side of the political spectrum, or can, at least, turn their back on leftist values. Examples include the "Yellow" union movement in the early twentieth century, for example, or the racist riots that took place in the south of France in the same period, or strikes opposing the hiring of foreign workers, and so on.[12] There have been many theorists of the left who over many years have tried to understand these kind of phenomena: think of Gramsci in prison wondering in his *Prison Notebooks* why, when all the conditions seemed to be in place at the end of World War I for a socialist and proletarian revolution to break out in Italy, it came to nothing. Or, more exactly, it took place, but the result was that the Fascists came to power. Or think of Wilhelm Reich, who, in 1933 in *The Mass Psychology of Fascism*, sought to analyze the psychic processes that led the popular classes to show support for fascism. Consequently, the relation that seems obvious between the "working class" and the left may well not be as natural as some would like to believe. It might rather be based on a representation that has been historically constructed by various theories (such as Marxism) that have won out over other competing theories and so have shaped both our perception of the social world and our political categories.[13]

My parents, like other members of my family from the same generation, claimed to be leftists. ("People like us *are* the left," I would often hear said within our family circle, as if it couldn't be any other way.) This was before they began voting for both the extreme right and the right (if in a discontinuous fashion). My brothers, like a certain number of other family members from their generation, openly assert their affiliation with the right—after having voted for the extreme right for many years; indeed, they are astonished that this could surprise anyone. As soon as they were able to vote, they began voting against the left. Working class regions, once bastions of the left and especially of the Communist Party, have guaranteed—and continue to guarantee—a significant electoral presence for the extreme right. I'm afraid it's the case that there are some cruel disappointments—along with some rather scathing refutations of their ideas—in store for those intellectuals who, demonstrating their own class ethnocentrism as they project their own manner of thinking into the skulls of those in whose place they speak while claiming to be attentive to their words, go on and on about the "spontaneous forms of knowledge" of the popular classes. Perhaps their enthusiasm is enabled by the fact that they have never in their life encountered anyone who belongs to those classes, except perhaps while reading writings from the nineteenth century. It is precisely these kinds of mythologies and mystifications, perpetuated by a certain set of people (seeking to be applauded as the promoters of a new form of radicalism), that the left needs to shake off—along with the neoconservative currents I described earlier—if it wishes to understand the phenomena that are leading it to its downfall, and then to reverse the process. There is no such thing as the "spontaneous knowledge" of the dominated classes; or, more exactly, we could say that any such "spontaneous knowledge" has no fixed meaning that would tie it to this or that form of politics. The position that any individual occupies within the social world and within the field of labor is not sufficient to determine that person's "class interest" or their perception of that interest in the absence of any mediation offered by the theories provided by movements and parties, theories that furnish a way of seeing the world. It is these theories that give form and meaning to someone's lived experience at any given moment, and the same experiences can take on quite different, and even opposing meanings as a result of the theories or discourses to which people have recourse and on which they choose to rely.[14]

This is why a philosophy of "democracy" that is content simply to celebrate the primary "equality" of each and every person, and to rehearse the notion that each individual is endowed with the same "competence" as every one else, is in no way an emancipatory way of thinking (and it makes no difference if the authors themselves profess a certain astonishment at the fact that they find themselves putting forth such a "scandalous" idea). This is because such a philosophy never asks itself about the ways in which opinions are formed. It never inquires as to how the results of this "competence" can entirely change directions—for better or for worse—on a personal level, or on the level of a social group, according to place and circumstance, and according to the discursive configurations within which, for example, the exact same prejudices might either become an absolute priority, or else be excluded from the political register.[15] I would not want my mother or my brothers to have their lot drawn—and indeed, it's not something they would ask for either—in order to take part in ruling the City in the name of their "competence," equal to that of anyone else. The choices they would make would be no different from those they express in the way they vote, except that perhaps in this case they would be in the majority. If my reservations offend the sensibilities of those who dream of a return to the Athenian sources of democracy, so be it. However sympathetic their stance might appear, I find it highly disturbing to imagine what the results of it might be.[16]

On a related point, we might ask how one is to take into account the practical existence of "social classes" and of the conflictual nature of society, even of the objective "war" I spoke of in an earlier chapter, without falling into the magical or mythical invocation of the "Class Struggle" extolled these days by those who call for a "return to Marxism," as if political positions just followed on in a univocal and necessary way from social positions, as if they led inevitably to a conscious and organized confrontation between, on the one hand, a "working class" that is no longer "alienated" and is driven by a desire for socialism, and, on the other, a "bourgeois class"? Such invocations rely blindly on these reified notions and fantasmatic representations, ignoring the dangers they represent.

What we must make an effort to understand is why and how it is possible for the popular classes to think of the conditions under which they live sometimes as tying them necessarily to the left, sometimes as self-evidently placing them on the right. A number of factors need to be taken into account: the economic situation, both global and local, of course; transformations in the nature of work and the relations between individuals that these transformations create or undo; but also, and, I would be tempted to say, above all, the way in which political discourses, discursive categories, play a role in shaping the process of political subjectivation. Political parties play an important role here, even perhaps a fundamental one, because, as we have seen, it is by way of them that people who otherwise have no voice can speak—by way of spokespersons who speak on their behalf, but also in their place.[17] The role of parties is fundamental also because organized discourses are what produce categories of perception, ways of thinking of oneself as a political subject, and also define one's way of conceiving of one's own "interests" and of the ways of voting that correspond to them.[18] We would thus do well always to be thinking about the antinomy that exists, for people from the popular classes, between the ineluctable character (outside of rare moments of struggle) of having to delegate their voice, and the refusal to be dispossessed by those spokespersons in whom it finally becomes impossible for them to recognize themselves—to such an extent that they go looking for, and find, new ones. Indeed, this is why it is always of the utmost importance to be wary of parties and of their natural tendency to wish to assure their hegemony over political life, and the natural tendency of their leaders to wish to assure their hegemony over the boundaries of the legitimate political field.[19]

So we find ourselves back at the question of who has the right to speak, who takes part—and how—in decision-making processes, which is to say not just in the elaboration of solutions, but also in the collective definition of the questions that it is legitimate and important to take up. When the left shows itself to be incapable of serving as a space in which new forms of questioning can be elaborated and tested, when it ceases to serve as a locus in which people can invest their dreams and their energy, they will be drawn to and welcomed by the right and the extreme right.

Here, then, is the task that social movements and critical intellectuals must take up: the elaboration of theoretical frameworks and of political modes of perceiving reality that enable not an erasure—that would be an impossible task—, but as great a neutralization as possible of the negative passions that are at work within the social body, especially within the popular classes. Other perspectives must be offered and a different future sketched out on behalf of what might then deservedly once again be called the left.

IV

1

HOW DIFFICULT THEY WERE, my first years in high school! I was an excellent student, but always on the verge of giving up on school altogether. If most of the students at the school I attended had come from the same background as I did, and had not, as was actually the case, been children of the bourgeoisie and petite-bourgeoisie, I have little doubt that I would have done what the system expected of me and dropped out. Whenever there were students making trouble, I was part of it, arrogant and impertinent, constantly speaking back to my teachers, never hiding my scorn for them. My ways of speaking and of carrying myself, my behavior and the expressions I would use, must have made me seem like part of some lunatic fringe—a bad seed more than a model student. I don't remember quite what the verbal sally was that I had directed at one of my classmates, the son of a judge, and that earned me the outraged reply: "Curb your tongue!" He was dumbfounded by the verbal crudeness of working-class people, something he was not accustomed to, but his reaction, and the tone of voice in which he expressed it, both of them drawing on the linguistic repertory of his bourgeois family, seemed to me ridiculous, and only encouraged my irony and vulgarity. There was an implacable social logic that was turning me into this particular character, one I naively took pride in.

Everything seemed to be encouraging me to choose this role, one that had been held in reserve for me, linked to a fate that had always been lying in wait: a prompt exit from the educational system. When I was in sixth grade, a teacher said to me, "You'll never make it past the second year of high school." I lived in fear of that judgment until I actually made it into that year, and then through it. But, when you get right down to it, the idiot who said that to me had demonstrated a certain kind of clear-sightedness: it wasn't intended that I make it any further than that, or even that I make it that far.

I discovered in the short book that Pierre Bourdieu finished and sent to his German publisher a month before his death, *Sketch for a Self-Analysis*, a kind of blown-up image of what I had lived through. He portrays himself in that book as a pre-teenager and then a teenager "always in a state of revolt close to a kind of delinquency," and he describes the "clashes with school discipline" that ceaselessly produced in him an attitude of "stubborn fury" that nearly got him expelled from school just prior to the Baccalaureate examination. Yet at the same time, he was an exceptional student, devoted to his studies, spending hours quietly reading, shutting out all the commotion he regularly helped produce and the rows that he often provoked.[1]

Unfortunately, Bourdieu doesn't here push his self-analysis as far as he should have. He warns us on the first page of the book that, as a way of helping the reader understand him and his work, he will present the kinds of material "pertinent from the point of view of sociology … and only those." Yet we might wonder how he is able to decide for his readers which are the elements they need in order to grasp the dispositions and the principles that presided over the birth of his intellectual project and the development of his thought. Moreover, it is hard not to have the impression that the elements he foregrounds in writing of his youth, and his way of foregrounding them, belong more to the register of psychology than to that of sociology; it is as if he had wanted to describe the traits that made up his (difficult) personal character and not the logic of the social forces that acted on him as an individual. His writing is too reserved, too diffident—and doubtless the main function of his opening remark is to justify his caution and his parsimoniousness. He doesn't dare reveal himself any more fully, providing only fragmentary information and most certainly neglecting many key aspects. He leaves out more than he reveals.

For example, he does not explain how he managed to deal with the tension or the contradiction between his social ineptitude when it came to conforming to the demands of the school environment and his desire to learn and to succeed; nor does he explain how his desire in the end won out over his ineptitude (obvious traces of this ineptitude remaining visible much later on in his way of conducting his intellectual life, in his evident lack of respect for the rules of bourgeois decorum that reign in university circles and tend to impose themselves on anyone who does not wish to be excluded from the "scholarly community," rules that insist that people follow established norms regarding "intellectual debate" when what is at stake clearly has to do with a political struggle). He doesn't explain how he overcame all these difficulties and managed to survive in a universe that everything he was encouraged him to reject, even as he wanted nothing more than to remain in it. (For instance, he describes himself as "paradoxically so well adapted to the boarding school world which I so profoundly detested."[2]) It was this ambivalence that allowed him to become what he became and that inspired his entire intellectual project, as well as the approach he would take in the future: a rebellion—a "stubborn fury"— that continued in and through the production of knowledge. It is what Foucault, for his part, would call "intentional intractability" [l'indocilité réfléchie].

He doesn't mention any of the books he read; he tells us nothing about any of the people who were important to him, who gave him a taste for culture or for thought at a moment when he could simply have sunk into a complete repudiation of such things. The value placed on sports and on masculinity in the world of the popular classes, values he admits he fully subscribed to, would have seemed to destine him for just such a repudiation, although he does mention rejecting the anti-intellectualism of those who shared these values with him. And he points out that he watched all those who came from backgrounds similar to his disappear one by one, year after year, from the educational universe.[3] How and why did he survive? Is it enough, given that we know who he became, to recount in a few pages towards the end of the volume the scuffles, fights, and similar escapades he was involved in as a young man, opposing them to his equally real taste for study, for reading, for knowledge? If it was meant to be illuminating, then this portrait is incomplete. What about the transformation he went through as the years went by, changing from a child from a village in the Béarn disconcerted by "certain 'cultural features'" that he learned at school, into a student accepted into an elite Parisian preparatory program before being admitted to the École Normale Supérieure on the Rue d'Ulm?

And what about the matter of bilingualism (speaking Béarnese with his father and French at school), of the accent he devoted himself to correcting once he had moved to Paris (ashamed both of its class origins and its geographical ones), an accent that would occasionally crop up again here and there in conversation? What about sexuality? Is heterosexuality such a given that there is no point in even mentioning it, in pointing it out, if only in counterpoint to the passing description of a classmate who played the violin and who, because "he was recognized as homosexual," suffered from endless bullying on the part of the others, who thereby proved they weren't homosexual? (The story follows the classic opposition between aesthetes and athletes, with the athletes, in Bourdieu's version of the story, being the same boys he played rugby with and watched slowly being eliminated from the educational system.[4])

I cannot help thinking that Bourdieu's thought and his speech remained, to a large extent, a bit stuck in or determined by those very modes of perception, or, better put, by those same dispositions, long ago deeply inscribed in his very being—especially when, earlier in this same book, he comes close to designating Foucault in a pejorative manner as an "aesthete." For this is a label that, following the structuring polarities that he himself lays out in his final chapter, would send us back to the opposition between people who are "into sports" and "homosexuals," between the rugby team and the music lover; it sends us back to a certain social and sexual unconscious. When he had me read the manuscript of this text, I quite openly expressed my astonishment to him about the fact that he hadn't seen the homophobic nature of this unconscious.[5] This is another area in which his self-analysis could have been taken further. He emphasizes in the book, in the passage where he is endeavoring to make explicit how "I situated myself objectively and subjectively in relation to Michel Foucault," that he shared with him "almost all the pertinent properties," with a few exceptions: "Almost all —except two, but these, in my view, had very great weight in the constitution of his intellectual project: he came from a well-to-do provincial bourgeois family, and he was homosexual." Then he adds a third distinguishing feature, which is "the fact that he was and declared himself to be a philosopher," but this feature, he notes, was perhaps only an "effect of the first two." Bourdieu seems to me to be right on the mark here. There is no disputing what he says. But the inverse must then also be true: Bourdieu's choice of sociology, and even the very physiognomy of his work, could well be linked to his class origins and to his sexuality. Support for this could be found in the judgment he offers more generally of philosophy. Taking the side of sociology and of "science" against philosophy, he marshals a whole vocabulary that is structured by an opposition between masculine and feminine—something he should have been conscious of, given his masterful study of these binary oppositions not only in his studies of Kabylia, but also in his study of the academic field and its division into disciplines.[6]

If I was able in many ways to recognize something of myself in the description Bourdieu offers towards the end of his book of the tension that was so significant in his youth between his sense of not fitting in to the educational system and yet his ever deeper attachment to it, there was a major difference between my path through my high school years and his. Despite a few attempts, in my early days in the world of secondary education, to conform to the model imposed upon me by the values I had incorporated from my social milieu, it didn't last. I quickly left behind the various kinds of role-playing involved in affirming masculinity (the tendency to pick fights, which really didn't suit me, but which I had learned from watching my older brother and, more generally, the other men—and also women—in my family) and began rather to disassociate myself in ever more marked ways from the typical behaviors of young people from the popular classes. You could say that, having started out resembling the troublemakers from Bourdieu's story who refused to be studious, I would then make a concerted effort to resemble the fellow who played the violin, the "aesthete" who had no interest in being an "athlete," even if I was still actively involved in sports (although that was something I would soon give up in an effort to correspond more fully to what I wanted to be, even going so far as to regret that I had built up my body instead of letting it remain lanky, puny even, in accordance with the image I now had of what an intellectual's appearance was and should be). That is to say that I chose culture over popular virile values. A commitment to culture—a vector of "distinction," which is to say a manner for differentiating yourself from others, of creating distance between yourself and others—often constitutes for a young gay man, especially if he is from the working classes, a mode of subjectivation that allows him to sustain and give meaning to his "difference." Consequently, it can serve as a way of building a world, of constructing an *ethos* that is different from the one he inherits from his social circumstances.[7]

Learning to be studious, to be scholarly, with all that involves, was a slow and chaotic process for me: the discipline required—both of body and of mind—is not something one is born with. It takes time to acquire it if you are not fortunate enough for that acquisition to have been encouraged in you since childhood without you even being aware of it. For me it was a true process of ascesis: a self-education, or more exactly, a reeducation that involved unlearning everything I already was. What was a matter of course for others was something I had to struggle with day after day, month after month, working anew each day to find ways of organizing my time, of using language, of relating to others, that would transform my very person, my *habitus*. The process would place me in an increasingly awkward position within my family, to which I returned each evening. To put it simply, the relation to oneself that is imposed by scholarly culture turned out to be incompatible with the way people behaved in my world; the educational process succeeded in creating within me, as one of its very conditions of possibility, a break—even a kind of exile—that grew ever more pronounced, and separated me little by little from the world that I came from, the world in which I still lived. Like every situation of exile, my own contained a certain kind of violence. Perhaps I wasn't aware of it, given that I consented to having it inflicted upon me. In order not to shut myself out of the educational system—or to be expelled from it—I had to shut out my own family, the universe from which I came. There was really no possibility of holding the two worlds together, of belonging in any easy way to both of them. For a number of years I had to shuttle back and forth between two registers, between two universes. A split as agonizing as this one—between the two different persons I had to be, the two roles I had to play, my two social identities, less and less related to each other, less and less compatible with each other— produced in me a level of tension that was difficult to bear and, above all, highly destabilizing.

Attending the main high school in the city brought me into direct contact with the children of the bourgeoisie (and with the sons of the bourgeoisie in particular, since co-education had barely begun at this point in time). The other boys' ways of talking, the clothes they wore, and above all their familiarity with culture—by which I mean legitimate culture—all reminded me of my status as an intruder, as someone who was clearly out of place. Music class was perhaps the most insidious kind of litmus test, also the most brutal, of one's mastery of what was understood by "culture"—whether it was something you experienced as self-evident or as utterly foreign to you. The teacher would bring in records, and would play endless excerpts of various pieces to us. Students from bourgeois backgrounds would pretend to be caught up in some kind of inspired reverie. Students from the popular classes would whisper silly comments to each other, or would be unable to restrain themselves from talking out loud, or bursting into laughter. If you were one of those students who found it difficult to conform to the social injunction addressed to you and all the students in it by the educational system, through every bit of its machinery, then everything conspired to implant in you the feeling that you didn't belong, that this was not your world. In reality, there were only two paths open to me. I could continue to resist in an impulsive, unpremeditated kind of way—a resistance expressed in any number of rebellious attitudes, maladjustments, misfits, dislikes and sniggers, obstinate refusals. I would then find myself quietly kicked out of the system like so many others, because of the way things were set up, even though it would end up seeming to be due to my own behavior. Or I could little by little shape myself to what the school required; I could adapt, accept its demands, and thereby manage to remain within its walls. If I resisted, I was lost. If I gave in, I was saved.

DURING MY TIME IN HIGH SCHOOL, around the age of 13 or 14, I became close friends with a boy in my class who was the son of a college professor. (The local university was brand new at the time.) It would hardly be going too far to say that I was in love with him. I loved him as teenagers do. Yet, both of us being boys, there was no way I could tell him what I felt for him. (This is one of the more traumatizing kinds of difficulties tied to the experience of same-sex attractions during one's teenage years—or even at other moments in life: not being able to express what you feel for someone of the same sex. It explains why places where gay people can meet—once you find out they exist and once you are old enough to seek them out—take on such importance, for in them the prevailing under-standing of how certain kinds of things work is reversed.) I just wrote "there was no way I could tell him what I felt." Of course that's true. But even before that, it would have had to be possible for me to express those feelings to myself. I was still too young for that. The whole surrounding cultural universe was organized in such a way (and to a great extent it still is) that people of that age do not have access to references, discourses, images that would allow them to understand and name this particular kind of incredibly intense affective attachment as anything other than "friendship." One day, our music teacher asked us to try to recognize a piece he was going to play for us. I was flabbergasted when I saw this boy raise his hand after only a few measures and proudly announce, "It's Mussorgsky's *Night on Bald Mountain!*" Music class was one I had always found simply ridiculous, focusing on a kind of music I couldn't bear; I was forever finding ways to make fun of it, but I was also always trying to get this boy to like me, so I was totally thrown off balance by the discovery that he knew something about—that he enjoyed—something that seemed to me simply laughable, an object of scorn. At home, whenever we stumbled on a radio station broadcasting it, we referred to it as "fancy music," and quickly turned it off, saying "we're not at church."

His first name was a fine one, mine banal. That symbolized in some way the social gap that existed between us. He lived with his family in a large house located in a well-to-do neighborhood near the center of town. Whenever I went over to his house I was impressed and intimidated. I worried about him finding out that I lived in a new housing development on the edge of town, which meant I remained evasive whenever he would ask me questions on this subject. But then one day, probably just curious to find out where and how I lived, he came over and rang our doorbell unannounced. However kind a gesture it was, I was mortified, unable to grasp that he might simply have meant to let me know that I had nothing to be ashamed of. He had older brothers and sisters who were students in Paris and so (also because of the family atmosphere in which he was immersed) his conversation was filled with the names of directors and writers: he talked to me about Godard's films, Beckett's novels, and the like. I always felt ignorant in his company. He not only taught me about all these things, he also taught me to want to know about all of them. He fascinated me, and since I wanted to be like him, I too began talking about Godard, having never seen anything of his, and about Beckett, having never read a word. He was obviously a good student, one who never missed a chance to demonstrate a kind of dilettantish distance from the world of education; I tried to play the same game, without, of course, holding the same cards in my hand. I therefore learned how to cheat, pretending to know things I didn't. The truth didn't seem important. Appearances were what counted, along with the image I was struggling to construct for myself. I even went so far as to imitate the way he wrote (I mean his actual handwriting), and even today when I form the shapes of certain letters they carry the traces of this past relationship. But in fact, it wasn't a long one. I soon lost sight of him. It was the late 1960s, and the spirit of the time left a deep stamp on each of us, but a radically different one. He left school well before passing the Baccalaureate exam, and set out "on the road." He was a big fan of Kerouac's, loved playing the guitar, and was drawn to hippie culture. As for me, I was marked instead by the events of May 1968, by the political rebellion of that moment: in 1969, when I was barely 16 years old, I became a Trotskyite activist, and that took up most of my time for the next few years. I would remain active until about the age of 20, and this led me to read Marx, Lenin, and Trotsky. For me it was a decisive intellectual experience: it helped me set my sights on philosophy.

The influence this friendship had on me and the help that this boy offered me—without even realizing it—nonetheless had a defining impact. My class *habitus* had at first led me to resist acculturating to a life of study, to the kinds of discipline it required. I was unruly, intractable, and it wouldn't have taken much for certain irresistible forces to have pushed me over the edge towards a complete rejection of school. In his case, it was the opposite. Culture was his life, and always had been. He wrote short stories of a certain kind, in the genre of the fantastic. I set myself to writing, making an effort to imitate him. He had taken a pen name. I decided to do the same. When I told him what mine was, he made fun of me, for it was totally made up (preposterous and convoluted),whereas his, as he hammered home to me, was composed of his middle name and his mother's maiden name. There was no way I could compete with him. Everything I tried merely revealed my inferiority. He was cruel and hurtful without meaning to be, without even knowing it. In the years since then I have often come across situations like this: where a different class *ethos* lies behind certain behaviors and reactions that turn out to be nothing more than the putting into action of certain social structures and hierarchies within a specific interactive moment. Friendship cannot escape from the laws of historical gravity: two friends are still two incorporated social histories that attempt to coexist. And so sometimes in the course of a friendship, no matter how close, two classes come into conflict with each other, simply as the effect of the inertia of the *habitus* involved. Attitudes that are taken and words that are exchanged need not be meant aggressively, nor meant to be hurtful, and yet they may still be so. For example, when you spend time in bourgeois circles, or simply with ordinary middle class people, it is often simply assumed that you come from the same background. In the same way that heterosexual people always speak about homosexuals without stopping to think that the person to whom they are speaking might be a member of the stigmatized species that they are in the process of belittling or making fun of, so middle class people always address you as if your existential and cultural experiences have been the same as theirs. They don't even notice that they are attacking you by way of their assumptions (even if you are flattered and proud at managing to "pass" for something you are not—a child of the bourgeoisie—since you have spent so much time working to get yourself into this situation). Sometimes it happens even with your closest friends, the oldest and most loyal ones. When my father died, one of my close friends—an heir!—to whom I mentioned that I wasn't going to be attending my father's funeral, but that I nonetheless had to go to Reims to see my mother, made the following observation: "Of course. In any case you'll have to be there when the lawyer reads the will." These words, spoken in an utterly matter-of-fact tone of voice, reminded me of the truth of the fact that parallel lines never meet, even in the course of a friendship. The reading of the will? What will? Good heavens! As if anyone in my family drew up wills with their lawyers. What, precisely, would they be leaving to anyone? In the popular classes nothing passes from generation to generation, no securities, no capital, no houses or apartments, no antique furniture or valuable objects, nothing.[8] All my parents had were some meager savings, painstakingly accumulated over the years, and deposited in an account at a savings bank. And in any case, as far as my mother was concerned, that money belonged to her, since she and my father "put it away" together, setting aside a portion of their earnings that really would have come in handy for other basic things in life. The idea that this money, their money, would have to be passed on to anyone other than her, even if it was to her children, seemed inconceivable and unbearable to her. "But it's mine! We did without so much so that we could set that money aside for a rainy day…," she exclaimed indignantly upon learning from the bank that several thousand euros from their shared account would have to be paid to her sons, and that she was entitled only to a small portion of the account balance. She was thus required to ask us to sign a document conceding to her the proceeds of this "inheritance."

It remains the case that the boy I was friends with for this brief period in high school taught me to love books, taught me to think about writing in a different way, convinced me to become a believer in art and in literature—a belief I faked at the beginning, but that became more and more real as the days went by. What counted the most was really enthusiasm, a desire for discovery. The content of what would be discovered could come later. Thanks to this friendship, my kneejerk rejection to the world of studies—a reaction that came from my upbringing—didn't lead to a wholesale rejection of all forms of culture. It turned into a passion for anything avant-garde, radical, intellectual. (I was seduced by Duras and Beckett, but soon Sartre and Beauvoir would steal my heart from them. Given that I was mostly on my own in attempting to discover what authors and books to read, my choice would often be made after I saw that someone had signed a petition—especially during and after May 1968. That's how I came to buy Duras's *Destroy, She Said* in 1969 when it first appeared between what seemed to me to be the magical covers of the Éditions de Minuit. That's how, a bit later, I became fascinated by Beauvoir's memoirs.) So I moved with no transition from the readings of my childhood— I had eagerly read every volume of *The Famous Five* series published in the Bibliothèque Rose collection before entering high school—to the enthusiastic discovery of contemporary literary and intellectual life. I hid my ignorance, my lack of reading of the classics, the fact that I had read almost nothing that other people my age had already read—*War and Peace, Les Misérables*, and the like—feigning scorn and disdain towards my peers, taunting them for being conformist. They called me a "snob," which, obviously, left me overjoyed. I was inventing culture for myself, and at the same time inventing a character and a personality.

What has become of the person to whom I owe so much? I hadn't the slightest idea until a few months ago when I did a little research on the internet. We live in the same city, but on different planets. He continued to pursue music and has, it seems, built up a reputation in the world of the French *chanson* as an arranger of a number of successful records. It seems there is nothing to feel regretful about. What would we have had to say to each other once the period of our adolescent friendship had passed? It was a relationship that lasted only three or four years. I imagine it must have been much more significant for me than it was for him.

The educational choices I made also bear the mark of the deprived social circumstances from which I came. We had access to none of the necessary information regarding which tracks or classes were the preferable ones, had no command of strategies for seeking out prestigious subjects. I headed towards the literary track, whereas the smarter choice would have been a scientific one. (Those were the most sought-after classes at the time, but it is true that I had opted out of math classes just before high school and was drawn towards "literary" topics.) I had been a star student in Ancient Greek in middle school, but I dropped it before high school as well, managing to convince myself it served no purpose—but mainly because the boy I was just speaking about had decided to drop it, and I always conformed to his judgments regarding what to do or not to do—mostly because I wanted to be in the same class with him. I continued only with Latin, whose interest also seemed less and less obvious to me. And I chose Spanish as my second modern language instead of German, although in this case I did the opposite of what my "guide" did. German tended to be the choice of children from bourgeois families or whose parents worked in intellectual professions. The Spanish class gathered together the weakest students in the school, at least from an intellectual point of view, and also all the students from less privileged class backgrounds—these two characteristics being statistically linked—and so my choice, which really wasn't a choice, was in some way the prefiguration of a more or less direct long-term process of scholarly elimination, or else an assignment to one of those educational tracks born out of an effort at "democratization," tracks that served as a kind of educational dumping ground, making crystal clear that that so-called "democratization" of education was to a large extent illusory. I understood nothing of all this, of course, and simply followed my likes and my dislikes. I was drawn to the south, to Spain, and I wanted to learn Spanish. (As my mother recently reminded me, when I made fun of her biological fantasies regarding Andalusia: "But you know that you also talked about Spain all the time when you were little, and you had never been there. There must be a reason for it.") I detested Germany, and the German language. I found them repulsive. In this regard I was a Nietzschean before ever reading Nietzsche. I am thinking of *Ecce Homo* and *The Case of Wagner* in particular, where one finds the Mediterranean as a frame of reference: warmth against cold, lightness against heaviness, liveliness against seriousness, the joy of noon against the sadness of night. I believed I was making a choice, whereas in reality I was being chosen, or perhaps captured by what lay in wait for me. This was something I only realized when a literature teacher who showed some concern for my academic success pointed out to me that the choice of Spanish placed me in a lower track and obliged me to sit and vegetate among the worst students in the school. In any case, I figured it out soon enough: I was on the track followed by those who most resembled me socially, not the one followed by those whom I resembled intellectually. (What this reveals is that a child from the lower classes, even when he or she is an excellent student, is highly likely to make wrong turns and end up following the wrong educational path, which means always being shunted aside from, always being placed below, the tracks that represent high achievement, be it social or educational.)

So I came to my final year in high school in the literary track. Philosophy was one of the subjects, but the instruction I received turned out to be, alas, ineffectual, even ridiculous. The teacher may have been young (he had just passed the exam for his teaching certificate), but he was uninspired, and dealt with the topics on the program by dictating to us a lesson carefully divided up into paragraphs: "Subpoint number one, Bergson's thesis. Subpoint number two, the thesis of ..." On each topic he read us his note cards and offered insipid summaries of doctrines and of works that he probably only knew himself thanks to his reading of textbooks that covered them. Nothing was questioned critically; no problems were posed; there was nothing at stake. What he taught was without interest, and so no one took an interest in it. The books he liked and recommended to his students were ridiculous. (He lent a certain number of us Louis Pauwels's *The Morning of the Magicians*, and other nonsense of this nature!) I was keen to be introduced to critical thought, to theoretical reflection. His flat and routinized pedagogy acted like a bucket of cold water on my budding enthusiasm. It would have turned anyone away from philosophy. I never had the good fortune of coming into contact with one of those people whose teaching electrifies the classroom, a teacher you remember for the rest of your life, who introduces you to authors whose entire works you then immediately devour. No, he offered nothing except a colorless kind of boredom, and I skipped as many classes as I could get away with. For me, philosophy was Marxism and the authors Marx cited. By reading Marx I became passionate about the history of philosophical thought. I read an enormous amount, with the result that I ended up doing extremely well in philosophy on the Baccalaureate exam. The same was true in other subjects. (On the history exam, I was questioned about Stalin. As a Trotskyite, I knew everything there was to know.) I passed the whole exam without any problem. It was even easy. For my parents this was an unbelievable event. They were stunned.

When I went to enroll in the humanities and social sciences division at the university, I was torn between choosing English and Philosophy as my subject. I chose Philosophy, which seemed to me a better match with the image I had of myself, and which would henceforth be central to my life and to the shape of the person I would become. In any case, I took a lot of satisfaction from the choice I made. It gave me a kind of naive happiness to now be someone who was "studying philosophy." I had no knowledge of the existence of the prestigious Grandes Écoles in Paris, with their competitive entrance exams, nor of the preparatory courses for them, called *hypokhâgnes* and *khâgnes*. In my final year in high school, I didn't even know such things existed. It is not just access to these institutions that was, and still is (perhaps to an ever greater extent) reserved for students from the privileged classes. The simple knowledge that such possibilities exist is even unavailable to many, with the result that I never even considered them as a possibility. When, already enrolled at the university, I did finally hear people talking about these kinds of possibilities, it seemed to me—how naive I was!—that I was in a better position than anyone who would have chosen to continue studying within the confines of a high school—what a strange idea it seemed— after they had already passed the Baccalaureate exam, instead of immediately "going to university." That seemed to me the most obvious aspiration for any serious student. Here again we can observe how a simple lack of knowledge regarding the hierarchical structure of educational institutions and a lack of understanding of how processes of selection operate might lead someone to make counterproductive choices, to choose paths that lead nowhere, nonetheless imagining they are lucky to have gotten to a place in which people who know what they are doing would be sure never to end up. This is how people from less advantaged classes end up believing that they are gaining access to what has previously been denied to them, whereas in reality, once they have that access, it turns out to mean very little, because the system has evolved and the important and valuable place to be has now shifted somewhere else. The process of being pushed out or excluded may here be happening more slowly, or happening at a later date, but the division between those in dominant positions and those in dominated ones remains intact. It reproduces itself by changing location. This is what Bourdieu calls the "displacement [*translation*] of the structure."[9] What has been labeled a "democratization" is really a displacement in which, despite all appearances, the structure perpetuates itself, maintains itself with almost the same rigidity as in the past.

3

ONE DAY, AROUND THE TIME I started attending university, my mother said to me, and in a tone of voice that indicated that she had thought over carefully what she was going to say: "We can afford to pay for two years of college. After that you'll have to work. Two years is a good long time." In her eyes (as in my father's) it was an amazing privilege for someone to be able to continue studying at the university level up to the age of twenty. I was myself still mostly unaware that literary studies in a provincial university could be nothing more—or barely anything more—than a dead end. But I did know that two years was too short to lead to anything professional, since it took three years to get your *licence* and four for a *maîtrise*. I was captivated just by the names of these diplomas, having no idea that they were already starting to lose most of their value. Still, given that I wanted to become a high school teacher, I had to obtain them before I could sit for the recruitment exams for high school teachers: the CAPES, and then the *agrégation*. On top of that, I couldn't imagine leaving the university behind so quickly because I was so passionate about philosophy. Not, of course, the old fashioned, soporific philosophy I had been being taught, but rather the philosophy I had started teaching myself around that time, which is to say mostly Sartre and Merleau-Ponty. I was also fascinated by humanist Marxists from Eastern Europe, especially Karel Kosík, whose *Dialectics of the Concrete* I found especially beguiling. I remember absolutely nothing about the book now, except that I was so taken with it that I read it several times from cover to cover in the space of a few years. I also admired the early Lukács's *History and Class Consciousness* (while reviling the later Lukács of the 1950s, because of his Stalinist attacks on Sartre and existentialism in *The Destruction of Reason*), Karl Korsch and a number of other authors who supported an open, non-dogmatic form of Marxism. Another example was Lucien Goldmann, a sociologist who is mostly—and perhaps unjustly—forgotten these days, but who was extremely important at the time, and whose books, *The Hidden God* and *The Human Sciences and Philosophy*, I took to be masterpieces in the sociology of cultural works. I would pepper the papers I wrote with references to these authors, which must have seemed a bit odd to the reactionary professors for whom I was writing (two of whom had just co-authored a book titled *The Crime of Abortion*). They all were convinced, as one of them told me, that I was far and away the best student they had ever had, but they would inevitably return my papers to me with a score of 10 out of 20, even while praising the "originality of my thought." Time after time, it was a 10. They would occasionally bring themselves to give me a 12 when I played by their rules, more or less successfully, citing Lavelle, Nédoncelle, Le Senne, or some other author they were fond of. It was only in papers on the history of philosophy that I could really excel, even if it always seemed to my teachers that my version of Plato or of Kant was too much under the influence of the set of thinkers I was so enthusiastic about at the time.

Anyone who stumbled into this philosophy department, a place of demoralizing torpor and paralysis (different from the excitement that could be found in other areas of the same university), would find themselves in a universe closed in upon itself, one from which all the sounds and colors of the outside world had been banished. Time had ground to a halt, frozen for all eternity: here, May 1968 had never happened, nor any of the critical social and political thinking that had accompanied the important uprising of that moment. I had been hoping to discover past and present forms of thought in their relation to the world around me, and yet here we were, stuck writing tedious and redundant summaries of authors and texts that we would have been better off reading on our own; we would have understood better what they said and what could be done with them than did those who were being paid to teach them to us. It was intellectual pedantry at its worst. This was a time when new universities were being established or others were expanding all over France, and it seems likely to me that the standards used in appointing "teachers" (if they deserved to be called that) might have been a bit lax. It turned out to be a bad strategy for retaining students. They left in droves as the months went by; the wave of desertions was so strong that I almost got caught up in it at the end of my first year. And indeed this might be seen simply as an amplification of a more general phenomenon, to the extent that the same fate was lying in wait for a good portion of all the students from the poorer classes in any discipline who had managed to hold on for this long. Once the structure provided by high school was no longer in place, they were left on their own to organize their work habits, and they often didn't manage to establish good ones. In the absence of any pressure from their families to continue—indeed the pressure was more likely in the opposite direction—the system of elimination quickly set itself in motion yet again, this time making use of the centrifugal forces of loss of interest and of capitulation.

I was having a hard time finding my feet: at the end of the first year I only barely managed to pass my exams, and that was on the second try, in early September. But that experience woke me up a bit, so I decided to persevere. Even so, I liked to imagine that what I felt towards certain of my professors, the ones I was just speaking about, caricatural incarnations of a certain kind of academic mediocrity, must have been something like what Paul Nizan describes feeling for his professors at the Sorbonne in the 1920s and 1930s: anger in the face of the "watch dogs" of the bourgeoisie.[10] Yet in point of fact the two situations were not at all similar. The philosophers Nizan was taking on so mercilessly were all brilliant thinkers and eminent professors. They were teaching young people from the dominant social classes, and working diligently to justify for them a vision of the world favorable to the maintenance of the established order. As for my own professors, they were talentless tutors of a kind of culture they did their best to render useless, emptying it of any substance; they were utterly inept at preserving anything; they conveyed nothing to any of their students, none of whom, in any case, would ever find themselves in any position of power. They truly gave us nothing! Except, perhaps, by accident and as a reaction against them, a desire in a few of their students to look elsewhere, to read other things.

Obviously, the components making up my intellectual horizon were mostly beyond the ken of my professors, and this occasionally allowed for some comic moments. There was the day when I mentioned Freud in the course of one of my presentations, causing the objection to be offered that he "reduced everything to the level of man's lowest instincts." Or there was the time when, after I had made mention of Simone de Beauvoir, this same ultra-Catholic professor, an extremely powerful presence in the philosophy department, interrupted me and curtly interjected: "You seem to be unaware that Mademoiselle de Beauvoir treated her own mother disrespectfully." I imagine he was alluding to the beautiful *A Very Easy Death*, in which she recounts both the life and the death of her mother. "Mademoiselle"! I laughed for months each time I thought of this way of referring to her.

They served us up courses on Plotinus and Maine de Biran (about whom I understood next to nothing, and in whom I had a hard time finding anything interesting), but never on Spinoza, Hegel, or Husserl, who seemed not even to have existed for them. As for "contemporary philosophy," it never managed to advance beyond existentialism (which was taken up in one quite academic, but well-informed, course on "Bergson and Existentialism," where the professor demonstrated how much Sartre owed to Bergson's philosophy). In the four years I spent studying in this department, I never heard mention of Lévi-Strauss, Dumézil, Braudel, Benveniste, Lacan, and so on, even though their importance had been recognized for quite some time. Obviously authors like Althusser, Foucault, Derrida, Deleuze, and Barthes were never even mentioned even though they were all quite famous by now. But that was in Paris and we were in Reims. We may only have been 150 kilometers from the capital, but there was still a huge gulf separating us from intellectual life there, an intellectual life that had been in the process of reinventing itself with varying degrees of intensity ever since the end of the war. I do, of course, fully realize that my youthful philosophical enthusiasms were in fact tied to my provincial situation and my class position. What I experienced as a chosen preference for a certain kind of philosophical thought was really something dictated to me by my social position. Had I been a student in Paris, or at least not so distant from those locations in which new ways of thinking and new kinds of theory were being developed and celebrated, I would have chosen Althusser, Foucault, or Derrida, and not Sartre, whom I would have regarded with disdain. It was only a bit later that I would discover that being disdainful of Sartre was the done thing in Parisian circles, where people preferred Merleau-Ponty, who was taken to be more serious because he hadn't garnered the same degree of worldly acclaim. (Althusser emphasizes this point in his posthumously published memoirs.) Still, I remain convinced even today that Sartre is a much more powerful and more original thinker than Merleau-Ponty, who was more of a professor, a traditional academic, and whose approach for a long time—until the break between them—owed a great deal to Sartre. More generally, I would have made more of an effort to stay up to date with the most sophisticated of contemporary intellectual developments. But in the time and place where I found myself, Sartre for me had all the answers. As far as I was concerned, it was Saint Sartre. Looking back on this period now, I see no reason to regret my past enthusiasm. I prefer having been a Sartrean to having been an Althusserian. I should add that after a long period in which it seemed I had broken with those early intellectual loves of mine, my "existentialist" leanings would return as I formulated my own projects—in which references to Sartre's thought would intermingle and coalesce with references to my later readings in Foucault and Bourdieu.

Yet if I wanted to go on pursuing my interest in this thinker whom I found so captivating, I was going to have to earn a living. Many students had to find some kind of work to support themselves while they pursued their studies. I had no choice but to resign myself to doing the same if I wished to avoid having my aspirations toward an intellectual life crash into the wall represented by economic reality—a reality my family reminded me of nearly every day.

But then a roll of the dice came along to abolish that necessity. I'm not sure how I learned of this opportunity nor how I convinced myself I should try my luck, but in any case, at the end of my second year at university, I signed up for, and managed to pass, the IPES exam. (I think, though I am not certain, that it stood for *Institut pédagogique de l'enseignement secondaire*—the Pedagogical Institute for Secondary School Teaching.) The written portion of the exam was made up of an essay on a general topic and a commentary on a specific text. I have no recollection today as to what the topic of the essay was. I remember the commentary was on an excerpt from Schopenhauer's *The World as Will and Representation*. I had just read a number of books on Nietzsche that dealt with his relation to Schopenhauer, and, armed with this reading, I had no problem writing brilliantly on the assigned passage. The other candidates, who were probably disconcerted by the strangeness and the difficulty of the passage, had a harder time with it. When the results were posted, I was overjoyed to see that there was only one name on the list of people who had been passed on to the oral portion of the exam: mine. As the only one left in contention, I still had to pass two oral exams, but I was nearly there. At the orals, my mark in sociology was barely average, but in foreign languages—I had chosen English—I was able to translate a text by Marcuse perfectly and my commentary on it—in which I compared his idea of the "atomization" of individuals to Sartre's concept of seriality—won high praise from the woman from the English Department who was my examiner and who gave me a very high mark. I had successfully jumped the hurdle and was poised to become a "student-teacher": I would be paid a stipend for two years, or even three if I managed to get a high enough mark on my master's thesis (which I did). The most surprising thing about all of this was that nothing was to be demanded of me in return during the years I was studying. The only obligation was that I work in secondary education for ten years after passing the two recruitment exams (the CAPES and the *agrégation*). But at the time there were so few jobs on offer (I sat for the *agrégation* twice: the first time there were 16 openings, and the second time 14, whereas over one thousand people were taking the exam), that I had no chance of passing. To have had any chance of passing— and it's no different today, or the situation may even be more extreme—you would have needed to go to all the best schools, which would have involved taking the right preparatory courses so that you could get into the Écoles Normales Supérieures. My failure was a foregone conclusion. But this was something I would only learn much later. For the moment, all that counted was my new status and the happiness it gave me: I was going to be paid so I could devote myself to my studies.

I opened a bank account and, as soon as it had money in it, I took a room near the center of town. My parents were not pleased about this. They would have preferred that I continue living with them and that I "hand over my pay." Up to this point in time, they had supported me, and it was difficult for my mother to accept and to understand why I would leave home the very day that I began earning my own keep, instead of beginning to help them in my turn. This whole situation must have been disturbing for her, and she surely hesitated about what course of action to take. Even though I was still a minor at the time (you only became an adult at 21), in the end she gave in and did nothing to stop me moving out. Not long thereafter I decided to move to Paris. I was 20 years old, and it was like a dream come true. Fascinated by Beauvoir's memoirs and everything she described in them, I wanted to see all the places she and her friends went to, the streets she spoke of, the neighborhoods she described. Today I know that I was caught up in imagining a world of legend, a world that was somewhat mythological. Still, it was a marvelous myth to me, and I was hypnotized by it. These were really years in which intellectual life, and the way it was caught up in political, social and cultural life, exercised a magnetic pull; it made you want to be part of this world of thought. People admired the major figures of the intellectual world; they identified with them, and were eager to take part in the creative activity around them. People imagined their future self as an intellectual figure, someone who wrote books, and who exchanged ideas with others during heated discussions, someone who intervened in political matters in ways that were both practical and theoretical. I could say that the two big reasons I had for wanting to move to Paris were

Simone de Beauvoir's books and my desire to live freely as a gay man.

I was still enrolled in the university in Reims, because my stipend was being paid to me by its administration. This meant I came back almost every week for classes, or just to meet attendance requirements. I did my Masters degree there, writing an essay on "Self and Other in French Existentialism," in which I dealt with Sartre's early works, up to *Being and Nothingness*, and with their relation to Husserl and to Heidegger. I haven't kept a copy of the thesis, and have only the vaguest of recollections of what I said in it. I do remember that at the end of the introduction, I attacked Structuralism, specifically Lévi-Strauss and the Foucault of *The Order of Things*, whose major error was, as I saw it in those days, that they "denied history." I hadn't read either of them; I simply rehashed all the commonplace attacks being made against them in those days by the Marxist writers who constituted my frame of reference, especially Lucien Goldmann and, above all, Sartre, who never stopped reasserting the freedom of the subject in the face of structuralist thought, although he started calling what he was defending "praxis" in his texts from the 1960s. He was endeavoring to rework (and thereby to preserve) the philosophical principles he had defined in *Being and Nothingness*, reconciling them with his later allegiance to Marxism, trying to make a place for forms of historical determinism while maintaining the ontological idea of the fundamental wrenching free of consciousness—his word was "nihilation" [*néantisation*]—from the weight of history and from the logic of systems, from rules and from structures.

I was awarded my degree with honors, and thanks to the extra year of IPES funding that I thereby obtained, I left this university behind (it really was, at the time, third rate), enrolling for an advanced degree (a DEA, *diplôme d'études approfondies*) at the Sorbonne (Paris-I), while also studying for the *agrégation*. For reasons that now escape me, I was no longer required to be enrolled in Reims, even though the administration there still paid me my stipend. Perhaps this was because the DEA was considered to be the first year of thesis writing and so it was no longer deemed necessary to adhere to one's geographical assignments on the "academic map." I had already been living in Paris for two years, and now I would finally also be a student in Paris! Reims was behind me. I had no reason to be going back there, so I didn't. My life was in Paris, and I was happy there. At the Sorbonne, my professors were good ones, excellent and even inspiring. The difference between the Sorbonne and Reims was the difference between night and day. I would attend courses given by a number of these professors for two or three years. You might say that this was actually the moment when I became a student of philosophy. I had a lot of catching up to do—as was made clear to me each day as I compared myself to the students sitting next to me in the lecture halls. I therefore spent my time reading. One might say I was finally getting a philosophical education that had been long postponed. I threw myself into it body and soul: Plato, Descartes, and Kant took on a new light for me, and I was finally able to study Spinoza and Hegel in a serious way.

My DEA was a success. I wrote on Nietzsche and language. (What did I say? I have no idea. I don't think I kept a copy.) And, of course, I failed the *agrégation*, as anyone could have predicted. I wasn't too upset, since I hadn't really expected to pass. I had understood that I wasn't at the level required for a competitive exam like that.

I enrolled to begin working on a thesis. My topic had to do with philosophies of history from Hegel to Sartre's *Critique of Dialectical Reason*. It didn't occur to me to extend my topic far enough to include Foucault's *Discipline and Punish*, which had just appeared. I had no desire to read it. It didn't even cross my mind that I might do so. I would discover the emerging work of Pierre Bourdieu a little bit after this, and only then would I discover Foucault's work, which was already quite well established. My theoretical universe would be turned upside down. The result would be that Sartre was pushed into a back corner of my brain. It would only be fifteen years later that he would reemerge from the purgatory to which I had consigned him in my mind.

But if I wanted to be able to write my thesis and to make another attempt at the *agrégation*, I was going to have to find a job. After failing the *agrégation* exam the first time, at the end of the year in which I completed my DEA, my status changed. I would no longer be receiving a stipend, so I would need to figure out how to earn some money. I began working as a night watchman several times a week at a hotel in the rue de Rennes. (I finished my shift at 8 a.m. and would go directly to class at the Sorbonne, before going home to sleep in the afternoon. It was exhausting, and I only managed to keep it up for a few months.) Then I found work in the evenings, from 6 p.m. to midnight, in a nearby suburb. I kept an eye on computers. In those days they looked like tall metal cabinets, and I was in charge of backing up the data that churned through these machines by recording it on magnetic tapes the size of movie reels. At midnight I would run to the train station to catch the last train back to Paris. The work was totally without interest, but at least it left me time to read, and I devoted the time I was shut up in that office to the intensive study of the authors on my program. (In my mind's eye I can see myself spending entire evenings reading Descartes and Leibniz.) When, even though I did pretty well on the written portion of the *agrégation*, I nonetheless failed it for a second time, I became a bit desperate. I had gotten my hopes up and had put a lot of energy into my preparations for the exam. I had also invested a huge amount of time and energy into the idea of becoming a high school teacher, and now it had come to nothing. The national education system had turned me down. They were also unable to find me a position as a substitute (with no security of employment), which meant that I was no longer under any obligation to spend ten years working as a teacher. But I also didn't have the necessary means to keep pursuing my studies in the hopes of a university career. I had come to understand how obvious it was that only the "inheritors," people coming from certain kinds of social and economic privilege, could truly count on taking up such a career. I had run away from the place I came from, but now my origins caught up with me: I was going to have to give up my thesis, my intellectual ambitions, and all the illusions on which they were based. The truth that I had been trying to deny about what I was had reasserted itself and was imposing its consequences: I had to find a real job. But how? And what kind of job? We can see here how the value a diploma actually has is tightly correlated to the social position of the person to whom it belongs: my DEA had not been a gateway to a thesis for me, as it would have been for others. This was because you needed to have money to live on while you wrote a thesis. (Without it, you might stubbornly hold on to the idea that you were writing a thesis until the moment came when you finally had to admit the obvious: you hadn't been able to write a thing because you were too busy working and had no energy left for anything else.) On top of that, and here I'm simply pointing out something so obvious that there's no need to spend much time proving it, such a diploma does not have the same worth, will not open the same doors, for people who lack social capital or for people who don't possess the information that is needed to strategize about how to convert the diploma into a professional possibility. In these kinds of situations, help from families, relatives, friendship networks, and the like all contribute to the value a diploma is able to have when you are looking for a job. As far as social capital is concerned, it has to be said that I really didn't have much. Or, to be absolutely precise, I didn't have any. And as for strategic information: none of that either. Taken altogether, this meant my diploma was worth nothing, or next to nothing.

V

1

WHEN I THINK BACK over the years of my adolescence, Reims appears to me not only as the place from which I had to uproot myself, leaving behind my family and my class origins in order to live differently; it also figures as a town of insults. This fact also weighed heavily in the decisions I made. On how many different occasions was I called a faggot or some other similar word? It was an insult that became my constant companion, from the very first time I heard it. Yes, of course, it was a word I had always known in some way. Who doesn't? You learn it in learning to speak. I heard it at home and also outside my family circle long before I even knew what it meant.

I mentioned earlier that my father would often verbalize his anger at political figures who appeared on television as he was watching. The same was true when he would find himself confronted by people he couldn't stand because of their sexuality—real or imagined. If Jean Marais's name appeared in the credits for a film, every five minutes we would hear him repeat "fruit," "faggot," "fairy." The fact that my mother never missed a chance to remark that she thought he was handsome only made matters worse. She didn't approve of this kind of talk and so would make a point of replying, "What business is it of yours?", or "It's none of your business what other people get up to." Sometimes she would take a different tack and reply, "Maybe he is, but he's a lot richer than you are." Discovering little by little what my desires were, and what my sexuality would be thus meant inserting myself into a predefined category, one that had been stigmatized by means of these words of insult. It meant experiencing the terrorizing effect these words can have on those to whom they apply, on those who run the risk of exposing themselves to them for an entire lifetime. To use an insult is to cite the past. It only has meaning because it has been used by so many earlier speakers: "a dizzying word that rises from the depths of time immemorial," as one of Genet's verses puts it. Yet, for those at whom it is aimed, it also represents a projection into the future: the dreadful presentiment that such words, and the violence they carry, will accompany you for the rest of your days. To become gay is to become a target, and to realize that you already potentially were such a target even before you had actually entirely become one, before you were ever fully aware of what this word that you had heard hundreds of times might mean, even if you had always known how powerfully insulting it was. The stigmatized identity precedes you, and you step into it, you embody it, you have to deal with it in one way or another. They may be numerous and diverse, all the different ways it is dealt with, but they are all marked by the constitutive power of the verbalized insult itself. So it is not, as Sartre would have it in an enigmatic phrase he writes about Genet, that homosexuality is a way out that someone invents in order to avoid suffocating. It is rather that someone's homosexuality obliges them to find a way out in order to avoid suffocating. I can't help thinking that the distance that came into being—that I created—between myself and the world I grew up in, that my self-creation as an "intellectual," represented the way I found to deal with what I was becoming. I couldn't become what I was becoming without *inventing* myself as different from those from whom I was in fact already different. A bit earlier in this book, discussing my path through school, I described myself as a miracle case. It could well be that what made that miracle possible for me was my homosexuality.

Thus even before I discovered that this particular insult was referring to me, I was quite familiar with its use. I used it myself more than once. To be honest, I continued using it against other people even after I knew it was applicable to me. This would have been when I was around 14 or 15, and I did it as a way of protecting myself. I would, along with two or three other classmates, make fun of another boy in our high school whom we considered to be too effeminate. We called him a "fairy." By insulting him, I indirectly insulted myself, and, sad though it is to admit it, I knew this to be the case at the time. I was driven to it by an irresistible desire to belong to the "normal" world, to avoid paying whatever the cost was of being excluded from that world. It was probably also a way of lying to myself as much as I was lying to others, an attempt at a kind of exorcism.

Soon enough, in any case, the insult would come directly at me; people would use it specifically against me. I would be surrounded by it. It wouldn't be going too far to say that I was defined by it. It followed me everywhere, a constant reminder that I was breaking the rules, that I wasn't normal. The insult was always lurking outside the high school I attended or in the neighborhood where I lived, waiting to leap out. And leap out it inevitably would. When I would be visiting a cruising area (after I discovered around the age of 17 that such places existed)—

and in this case it wasn't a particularly discreet location, a street between the Great Theater and the Hall of Justice—a car full of idiots would slow down as it drove by so they could yell "faggots!" at everyone who was there. It felt as if there was some kind of organized conspiracy that had decided that this form of verbal aggression would only be strong enough and effective enough if it was repeated constantly and if it was found everywhere. It was something you had to learn to live with. What else could be done? But in fact I never really did manage to get used to it. Each time that same constantly reiterated insult was used against me, it seemed to stab me like a knife, and left me shaking with fear, since it meant that people either knew or suspected what I was—something I had been trying to hide. Or it meant I was being assigned to a certain fate, that of always being subject to this omnipresent denunciation, to the curse it pronounced. I was put on public display: "Look at him. See what he is. Did he think we wouldn't notice?" It was in fact the whole of the cultural universe around me that was calling me a "faggot," or else a "fairy," or a "fruit," or a "queer," or other ugly words that, when I hear them again today, reawaken in me the memory I have never been able to shake of the fear they provoked in me, the wounds they inflicted, the feelings of shame they drummed into my mind. I was produced by insult; I am the son of shame.

You might want to insist to me that it should be desire that comes first, that shame comes after, and that it is desire we should be speaking of. It is true that one becomes the object of insult because of the desire one feels, the kind of desire that insult denounces. And I did feel desire for boys in my classes, in the rowing club to which I belonged for a few years (from age

13 to 15), in the political organization in which I was active starting at the age of 16. My first sexual experiences were, in fact, with two boys from my rowing club and then with a class-mate my second to last year in high school. There were never any experiences with any of the other boys in the Trotskyist organization I've spoken of. Even if this organization didn't participate in the generalized homophobia that ruled over the Communist Party or over Maoist organizations, Trotskyist political organizations were fundamentally heterosexist and not in any way welcoming to homosexuality. You could often hear activists spouting a Reichian catechism regarding the "sexual revolution," a kind of Freudo-Marxism in which the traditional Marxist condemnation of homosexuality was mixed together with a Freudian one. The idea was that bourgeois society was built on the repression of libido, on the redirection of libidinal energy into work, and that consequently sexual liberation would contribute towards the creation of a new social and political system. But this way of thinking contained within it a disparaging evaluation of homosexuality, which was considered to be simply the effect of sexual taboos, something that would disappear along with them. The reality was that every day I had the feeling of there being no place for me within the Marxist world; when I found myself moving within this context I had to live a divided life, just as I did everywhere else. I was split in two: half Trotskyist, half gay. The two identities seemed irreconcilable; as time passed, I was having more and more difficulty reconciling them with each other, and it was becoming harder and harder for me to hold them together. It is easy for me to see why the gay move-ment of the 1970s found it necessary, as it was in the process of establishing itself, to break with these kinds of organizations and

with this kind of political thinking. Even so, the gay movement did remain—or parts of it did—heavily marked by Reichian ideology.[1] A large part of Foucault's aim when he undertook to write his *History of Sexuality* in the mid-1970s was to critique this Freudo-Marxian discourse. As part of a more general opposition to Marxism and to psychoanalysis, Foucault wished to forge a new approach to the question of power and of social change, freeing critical thought and radical liberation movements not only from Freudo-Marxism, but also, and he was equally firm about this, from Marxism and from psychoanalysis, from the "communist hypothesis" and from the obstacle that was Lacanian thought.[2] The return of these old, rigid, sterile dogmatisms on today's intellectual scene is something truly deplorable and represents a dangerous kind of regressiveness. They are, of course, often hostile to the gay movement and to sexual liberation movements in general. Their return to today's intellectual scene seems to be connected with and solicited by the reactionary moment we have been living through for many years now: they are simply the other side of the same reactionary coin.

In any case, these desires—my desires—along with the rare instances in which they were actually realized, had to remain silent and secret. What is a form of desire that must remain silent, hidden, publicly disavowed, that lives in fear of being mocked, stigmatized, psychoanalyzed, and then, once it has moved beyond this stage, must constantly affirm itself, reaffirm itself, and loudly declare its right to exist, sometimes in a manner that is theatrical, over the top, aggressive, extreme, one that seems to proselytize in an activist way? Such a desire carries within itself an essential fragility, a deep awareness of its own vulnerability, something it experiences at every moment and in every place. It is a desire that is filled with anxiety (at work, in the street, etc.). Things are only made more difficult by the way in which insult extends to include all the pejorative, devalorizing, derogatory, sarcastic, humiliating words that you hear without them even being addressed to you—the word "faggot" and all its synonyms that keep coming back obsessively in the conversations that make up daily life, in elementary school, in high school, at home... You feel yourself struck by these words, burned, frozen, even if those who use them in chatting with you don't seem to have any idea they might be talking about you. Inside yourself you experience these words as addressed to you even if they seem to be directed at someone else, or used in some general manner to refer to some category of persons to which you feel like you might belong, even if your most ardent desire would be not to do so. (This is surely one of the most powerful psychological mechanisms that contributes to producing the will towards disidentification that is so strong and so durable in many gays and lesbians. It also contributes to the sense of horror certain of them experience when confronted with the very existence of a gay and lesbian movement that is struggling to establish a self-consciously public image of something such people would prefer remained cordoned off in the private sphere, where it can claim the benefit of a social "right to be ignored." Of course, their own personal experience must contradict this fantasy of being left alone. Within their own experience it must be clear on a daily basis to what an extent private and public spheres are inextricably mixed together, to what an extent the "private" itself is a production of the public sphere—that is to say, to what an extent a given psyche is shaped, even within its most private recesses, by the injunctions of sexual normativity.) Actual or potential insults—which is to say not only those one is actually subjected to, but also those one fears being subjected to and so acts in order to avoid, and even those violent and obsessive kinds of insults by which one is always and everywhere surrounded—henceforth constitute the horizon of one's relation to the world and to others. Being-in-the-world becomes actualized as a kind of being-insulted, being rendered inferior by the social gaze and by social forms of speech. The object of an inferiorizing act of naming is produced as a subject subjugated by the structures of the sexual order (of which insult represents only the sharpest point). This subject's entire conscious mind, as well as his or her unconscious (to the extent that it is possible to imagine a clear line of separation between these two tightly connected spheres) finds itself marked and shaped by what has turned out to be the very process through which a sense of self and a personal identity are constructed. The process thus obviously cannot be said to be purely psychological: it is more the insidious and effective action of sexual norms and the hierarchies they control—hierarchies that produce, day in and day out, our psyches and subjectivities.

2

REIMS WAS THUS ALSO, and during this same period, the city in which I managed with immense difficulty to become gay, which is to say, to begin living a gay life even before I had acknowledged myself as such or claimed any such identity. You see, it turns out that even as you are trying to persuade yourself that there is something you really should avoid becoming—a "faggot"—, you are at the same time, and quite intensely, trying to figure out how to become precisely that. How are you going to meet partners—for sex or for love? How are you going to make gay friends, people to whom you can talk freely? One day you learn there are places gay men go to cruise. I found this out in a very strange way, during the summer when I was 17 years old. I was spending that summer working in the office of an insurance company, and one of the women working there would endlessly make fun of her manager behind his back. I remember her laughing while she said to me, "What a nancy-boy! Go by the theater some night and you'll see him out cruising." This piece of information thus came my way connected to an insult that terrified me; despite that, it was an incredible discovery for me. It was certainly true that this boss was someone who at work liked to throw around what little weight he had; he was petty, authoritarian, and rude, and he was also the constant butt of jokes for the young women he supervised. He seemed to believe no one knew anything about his sexuality, yet his every gesture, his way of walking, his voice and his manner of speaking all loudly broadcast to anyone around him what he nonetheless seemed to wish to keep hidden from them. There are certain gay people so intent on hiding what they are that the problem of their sexual identity comes to occupy a huge part of their mind. He was such a person. He could not stop himself from talking about homosexuality, and was constantly telling jokes about it, or "amusing" anecdotes that were always slightly off color— doubtless ones current in the gay circles in which he moved—, and he really seemed to believe that by directing this crude humor against those he was so fearful of being associated with, he would remove all suspicion from himself. Over the years, I have not infrequently encountered this same kind of duplicitous attitude (it comes in several varieties), a kind of attraction-repulsion that leads many gay people (I put this in the present tense, because cases like this still exist) to talk about homosexuality constantly, but in an ostentatiously derogatory or disgusted way, in order to put some distance between them and the people to whom they are linked in so many ways. (We could perhaps say that the paradigmatic instance of this attitude, as André Gide took great pleasure in pointing out in his *Journal*, is to be found in both the work and the person of Proust—even though it hardly needs saying that other people who engage in this practice don't always produce results that attain the same high level that Proust's did.)

Simply learning that a place like this existed was for me a miraculous revelation, even if the revelation occurred simultaneously with the act of someone pinning an ignominious label on anyone who happened to be caught visiting such a place.

Filled with apprehension at the prospect that someone I knew might see me there—since that would mean that I too could be called a "nancy-boy"—, I nonetheless found myself immediately dying to go see what went on there and, maybe, to meet someone. That very night, or maybe the next one, I got on my moped and headed in to the center of town. I parked at a safe distance from the street in which men could be seen rapidly and furtively going down the short flight of steps leading to a public restroom. Others could be seen further down the street strolling back and forth, and still others could be seen sitting in their parked cars. Occasionally one of those car's engines would start up suddenly, and the car would drive off, followed by a second one, the two drivers seeking a place where they could chat unseen. I don't remember if any one came up to me the first night I went there, or if it happened later. In any case, this became my entry into the gay world, and also a way into the whole subculture associated with that world.

I never actually ventured into the restroom. It was an idea that disgusted me, but that also left me unsettled. I didn't yet know that public restrooms—"tearooms" is what they are called in gay slang—have a longstanding place in the history of gay cruising. Still, that street and the streets around it, the square in front of the theater, and, not far off, the area around the cathedral, became from this point on frequent sites in the landscape of my night life. I spent entire evenings there, walking around endlessly, or pretending to use the phone booth that was at the bus stop, so that no one would be able to imagine that I was actually out cruising. Sometime in the days following my "first time," the woman at work who had been my informant and who seemed to have a way of knowing everything that went on, remarked to me: "I saw you hanging around the theater ... Were you out cruising?" I fabricated some kind of an excuse: "Of course not, I was on my way to see a friend who lives in that part of town." But what I said was hardly believable; the tone of my voice must have shown how uncomfortable the question made me. In any case, her mind was made up, which isn't to say that she showed any hostility towards me. The insults she used so freely when she spoke arose from what we might call habitual homophobia. Probably, if I had had the courage that day to admit to her that I was gay, she would have assigned me to her category of "nancy-boys," and would have made fun of me behind my back, without in any way changing her sympathetic feelings toward me, nor the kind and friendly ways she had of showing me how she felt towards me whenever she could. There grew up between us a strange kind of relation in which distrust and a strange kind of complicity were mixed together: she knew what I was and I knew that she knew, and she knew that I knew that she knew, and so on. I was terrified that she would speak to others about what she knew—as, indeed, she surely did—, while she toyed with my fear by making certain kinds of allusions, leaving me hoping desperately no one else actually understood them. I had been hired for two months by this insurance company thanks to my brother's wife (or his wife-to-be, since they weren't yet married at the time), who also worked there. The idea that the woman who had discovered my secret might inform her left me petrified. Did she, in fact, tell her? It seems likely, although it never showed if she did. The end of the summer came quickly enough, after which I never saw her again. But I would often come across similar examples of this kind of situation in which the play of power and that of knowledge were tightly intertwined. I thought of this woman again when, twenty years later, I read Eve Kosofsky Sedgwick's analysis in *Epistemology of the Closet* of the "epistemological privilege" heterosexuals benefit from, the way they can manipulate their knowledge of what homosexuals are while those they scrutinize wish nothing more than to escape from their gaze. Reading the pages in which Sedgwick discusses these questions, especially in her dazzling chapter on Proust, stirred up many memories from my past.[3]

Reims also had a gay bar in those days, and many people preferred the discretion it allowed to the danger of being publicly visible while cruising on the street. Myself, I would never have dared enter the bar, even if I had been old enough. And in any case, partly due to a kind of leftist puritanism and partly to a kind of intellectual elitism (or what I took for such), I considered bars and nightclubs to be disreputable, or at least contemptible, pastimes.

These kinds of meeting places also serve as places of social interaction, places in which you learn how to function within a particular culture. Each conversation, be it with someone you end up picking up or with someone you don't want to pick up, or else with someone you see every time you go there and end up getting to know (but without knowing much about them), is part of the socialization process for a young gay man, a way of becoming gay, in the sense of absorbing a kind of informal culture. You hear gossip about who in town might be "one of us"; you learn codes of behavior, a lingo, specifically gay ways of talking (ways of speaking in the feminine, for instance: "Look at *her*!"), classic jokes, and the like.[4] By way of these passing conversations and informal discussions, by looking through the books and collections of music belonging to people you go home with, you acquire a whole set of references: books that mention homosexuality (this is how I first heard of Genet, and immediately began reading him, and also how I first heard of other less imposing writers), singers who are adulated by gay people (after one of my lovers played me the records of a singer he adored, Barbara, I, like so many others, became a huge fan of hers, learning later, or perhaps right then, that she was a gay icon), classical music and opera (these were unknown, distant continents for me at the time, ones that thanks to these early initiations and incitements, I would later come to explore with great fervor, going so far as to become a connoisseur who never missed a concert or performance, who bought several recordings of the same work, who read biographies of composers such as Wagner, Mahler, Strauss, Britten, Berg ...), and so on. During conversations like these you hear about other cruising places, and rush off to check them out, or you hear about gay life in Paris, and begin dreaming about it. Thousands of informal discussions happening night after night in such places, involving countless meetings between newcomers to these places and more experienced visitors, thus all come together in a way no one participating in them is really conscious of, so that all of these individual "initiations" collectively become the medium through which a cultural heritage is transmitted. (It is, of course, a manifold heritage, varied according to ages and to social class, one that shifts over time, and yet all together it forms the contours of a specific "culture," or, if you wish, a "subculture.") We could take a certain literature of "initiation"—thinking perhaps of Gide's *The Counterfeiters* or Jouhandeau's *Du pur amour* or *L'École des garçons*—as a metonymy or a metaphor for a much larger phenomenon—a process of subjectivation happening through teaching and apprenticeship. It is similar in some ways to how for Foucault, towards the end of his life, the relation between a director of consciences and a disciple in the philosophical schools of Antiquity would serve as a metonymy or a metaphor for, or simply as a roundabout way of thinking about, larger processes involved in certain forms of gay relationality.

In any case, we can say that cruising areas have served as a kind of school of gay life, and this is true, obviously, whether or not anyone had a clear awareness of what was going on while the transmission of knowledge was actually taking place. In *Gay New York*, which covers the period from 1890 to 1940, George Chauncey provides a magnificent portrait and theorization of what I have been trying to describe here, and my description owes a great deal to what his work helped me to appreciate and to understand more fully.[5] Reading his book in the mid 1990s, I rediscovered so many things I had experienced in Reims in the late 1960s and early 1970s that I felt myself being caught up in a strange and dizzying experience of the intemporality—I almost wanted to say the universality—of homosexual experience. This seemed paradoxical, since the goal of Chauncey's book was to historicize the gay world, and along with it the sexual categories that govern it and the social and cultural practices that organize it and enable it to exist. Chauncey's intent is to show both that gay culture didn't wait until the Stonewall Riots and the late 1960s to come into existence, and that it was a notably different culture in the years he studies from the one we know today. *Gay New York* is a stirring work when it is read as an homage to all those who struggled to live their lives as they wished, to have a livable life—it is a hymn to a kind of gay resistance that operated on a daily basis, obstinate, tenacious, and inventive in its opposition to the power of dominant culture, a power that was always a threat, ready to abuse gay people, humiliate them, repress them, to track them and hunt them down, to strike them, wound them, arrest them, and put them in prison. Indeed the most important phenomenon Chauncey analyzes, the point of departure for his whole project (which reveals the strong influence on him of the urban sociology developed by the Chicago School), is the city: the way large cities attract gay people and the ways those people find to ceaselessly create and recreate the conditions necessary for them to be able to live out their sexuality: how they construct spaces of freedom, and how they put together a gay city within the straight one. This is not to say, of course, that gay life only exists within big cities! There are also places where gay people meet in small towns and in the country, along with forms of sociability and relationality that, even if less numerous, less concentrated, and less visible, are no less real for all that. But they exist on a reduced scale. In any case, in Chauncey's book I could read again the story of many of my own experiences or ones I witnessed. Above all, I found reconstituted in his book, under the rubric of the "gay world," the whole set of day-to-day practices, the whole set of multiple processes that allow one to put together a gay life alongside the other social life one also leads, a life in which it is preferable not to be identified as gay. This gay world and these gay ways of life do not have simply to do with "sexuality"; they also relate to the social and cultural creation of oneself as a subject. They could be described as the places, the means, the modes of a process of subjectivation that is at one and the same time individual and collective.

There surely are geographies and temporalities that are specifically gay or queer, as much wonderful recent work encourages us to imagine, having to do with where and how those people who somehow fail to correspond to the "norm" live their lives. It is just as true that those people whose existence is partially defined by these other space-times cannot live permanently within them. What characterizes queer lives or gay lives would rather be the capability—or the necessity—of moving regularly back and forth between spaces and between temporalities (from normal to abnormal and back again).

3

ANOTHER THING YOU ENCOUNTER in gay cruising places is violence—of many kinds. You meet strange people, people who seem half crazy, and you learn you must always be on your guard. Above all, you run the risk of physical attack by gay bashers or of being stopped by the police, who practice a certain kind of harassment in these places. Has anything changed on this front? I doubt it. I remember the dread I felt the first time I was stopped by the police—I must have been 17—and was told that I was mentally ill and needed help, that they were going to inform my parents, that I would have a record for the rest of my life. This was only the beginning of a long series of interactions with the police, always involving insults, sardonic comments, threats of various kinds. After a few years of this, it didn't bother me quite so much: it was just one among many features of my night life, not the most pleasant, obviously, but not particularly significant (at least for someone like me, since the risk is evidently much greater for someone who lives in a small town where everyone knows everything, or for someone whose papers are not in order). Gay bashings are more serious, and I was a victim of this extreme form of homophobic violence on a number of occasions. While I was never hurt too seriously, I knew someone back then who lost the use of one eye after being beaten by a group of thugs who were out to find some fags to bash. I should also mention here the endless acts of aggression to which I was a helpless witness over the years. After such events, you are left to turn them over and over again in your mind in the days and weeks that follow, relieved in a cowardly way that it wasn't you, but sad and disgusted at the fact of having witnessed one of these episodes of brutality that gay people must always worry about encountering, and in the face of which they are often so helpless. More than once I found myself suddenly running away from some place, barely escaping the fate that was about to fall on others. One day, shortly after moving to Paris, I was walking in one of the open areas of the Tuileries Gardens, one of the cruising areas I liked to visit after dark and which was always crowded, when I saw a group of young people coming from a ways off and obviously looking for trouble. They decided to pick on a somewhat elderly gentleman, roughing him up, punching him, and then, once he had fallen to the ground, kicking him. I saw a police car passing on the avenue that in those days ran along the edge of the park and I shouted for it to stop: "Someone is being beaten up in the park!" They replied, "We've got no time to waste on faggots," and continued on their way. Whatever city or town I would find myself visiting, for whatever reason, if I was out walking in a cruising area, I would witness similar scenes: gangs ruled by hatred suddenly descending on the area, forcing everyone there to flee, with the unlucky ones getting beaten up and often, though not always, robbed as well: watches, wallets, passports, and even clothes, especially if it was a leather jacket.

Gay spaces are haunted by the history of this violence: every path, every park bench, every nook that is sheltered from prying eyes carries somewhere within it all of this past, and also this present, and probably even the future of such attacks, along with the physical wounds they have left, are leaving, and will continue to leave behind (not to mention all the psychological wounds). And yet these spaces endure: despite everything, despite all one's own painful experiences or all the painful experiences of others that someone may have witnessed or heard tell of, despite all the fear, people keep coming back to these spaces of freedom. And so they go on existing, because, despite all the danger, people choose to keep them in existence.

It is true that internet dating services have profoundly changed the way people connect with potential partners and, have, in more general ways, profoundly changed the patterns of gay sociability, and yet it of course remains the case that nothing of what I have just described has disappeared. When I happen, not all that infrequently, to read a news story about a man found dead in a public park—or some functionally equivalent space: a parking garage, a wooded area, a highway rest stop—, a place that is "known to be frequented by homosexuals at night," I remember all of these scenes and experience once more all these feelings of rebellion and of incomprehension: why should people like me be subject to this kind of violence? Why are we obliged to live under this kind of permanent threat?

To all of this we need to add other forms of social devalorization and medical pathologization (such as we find at work in psychiatric and psychoanalytic discourses on homosexuality), which represented a different kind of assault. It was not a physical one, but a cultural and discursive one, and one whose prevalence, not to say omnipresence, in the public sphere was part and parcel of a generalized homophobia that many experienced as specifically targeted at them. Things are not that different nowadays, as was made obscenely obvious by the bigoted attacks that were unleashed in the debates concerning legal recognition for same-sex couples and for same-sex parenting: so much of what was written by those pretending to some kind of expertise—psycho-analytic, sociological, anthropological, legal, and so on—seemed to reveal itself as nothing other than the continual churning of the wheels of a political and ideological machine whose function is to ensure the perpetuation of the established order, the perpetuation of certain norms of subjection, to ensure that the lives of gay men and lesbians remain in an inferior situation, to keep the people living these lives in a state of self-doubt, one manufactured by the culture as a whole, a state from which they are today struggling to free themselves.

Why is it that a certain number of people seem committed to the hatred of others (whether it be expressed brutally through physical violence in cruising areas or in a more disguised way through acts of discursive aggression originating in pseudo-scientific or intellectual arenas)? Why is it that certain categories of the population—gay men, lesbians, transsexuals, Jews, blacks, and so on—have to bear the burden of these social and cultural curses, ones whose motivations and whose ability to perpetuate themselves seem so hard to fathom? This was a question I found myself asking over and over again: Why? And also: What did we do to deserve this? There is no answer to these questions other than the absurdity and arbitrariness of social verdicts—just as in Kafka's *The Trial*, there is no point in looking for the legal authority behind such judgments. It cannot be found; it does not exist. We are brought into a world in which a sentence has already been pronounced, and we come, at one point or another in our lives, to occupy the place of those who have been exposed to public condemnation, those who live with an accusatory finger pointed at them, who have no choice but to try to protect themselves from this condemnation, to do their best to manage this "spoiled identity," to quote the subtitle to Erving Goffman's books on *Stigma*.[6] This curse, this sentence that one has to live with, produces feelings of insecurity and vulnerability in the deepest regions of the self, and is the source of a diffuse kind of anxiety that characterizes gay subjectivity.

All of this, which is to say all these kinds of lived realities that are experienced from day to day and from year to year—the insults, the attacks, the discursive and cultural violence—is engraved in my memory (I am tempted to say: in my body). It is a key feature of gay lives, as it is of the lives of any stigmatized and minority subject. It can help us to understand, for example, the predominant climate to be found throughout Foucault's early publications in the 1950s, from his 1954 preface to the Ludwig Binswanger volume, *Le Rêve et l'existence* [Dream and existence] (where, in his interest for existential psychiatry, he seems so close to the Sartrean Fanon of *Black Skin, White Masks*, which had been published two years earlier) through *Madness and Civilization*, which was finished in 1960. It is a climate of anxiety, expressed in the vocabulary he mobilizes with a troubling degree of intensity, a vocabulary of exclusion, of alien status, of negativity, of enforced silence, a tragic vocabulary, a vocabulary of a fall. Foucault in some ways took a page out of the book of Georges Dumézil, who liked to place his research under the sign of the god Loki—a member of the Scandinavian pantheon known for his sexual transgressions and his rejection of the established order. Dumézil described Loki as an ideal psychiatric client, a classic psychiatric case, and he meant this as a compliment. If Foucault undertook to study the "Hell" of human "negativity" and of "anxiety" that medicine seeks to interrogate and regulate and reduce to silence, it was, in a manner related to Dumézil's, in order to shed light on this hell, to give the stammers one can hear there the means to express themselves fully.[7]

When I reread these incandescent but painful texts by Foucault, ones that stand at the beginning of his body of work, I recognize something of myself in them: I lived through what he writes about, something he had lived through before I did and was seeking a way to write about. Even today each of these pages provokes an emotional response in me, one arising from the deepest regions of my past; they give me the immediate feeling of an experience that I shared with him. I know how difficult it was for him to overcome these difficulties. He attempted suicide several times and walked a precarious line between sanity and madness for many years. (Althusser gives a superb account of this in his autobiography, speaking of this person whom he knew to be a brother in "suffering.") If Foucault did manage to work through these difficulties, it was by exiling himself (first to Sweden) and then by the patient effort of calling radically into question the pseudo-scientific discourse of medical pathologization. He set up the cry of Unreason (a category that includes both madness and homosexuality among other kinds of "deviance") in opposition to the monologue uttered by psychiatry (by which he designates discourse about normal people and normality) as it deals with those it takes as its "objects" and attempts to keep in a subordinated position. All of Foucault's political effort during this period was organized around a confrontation between exclusion and access to speech, pathologization and protest, subjugation and revolt.

Madness and Civilization can be read as a major book of intellectual and political resistance, as the insurrection of a subjugated subject against the powers of the norm and of subjection. As his work progressed, across all its many reformulations, Foucault would never stop pursuing this same goal: to think about the confrontation between a subject and the power of the norm, to reflect on the ways in which an existence can be reinvented. It is thus no surprise that his readers connect with his texts on this point (or at least certain of his readers do, since others see nothing more in them than fodder for academic commentary): this is because a certain set of readers feel that the texts are speaking about them, are addressing the rifts and fault lines that traverse them, which is to say the sources of their fragility, but also the sources of the restiveness and insubordination that can be born of these same conditions.

There's no doubt that we can include *Madness and Civilization* in that part of our library that includes books that "call to us," as Patrick Chamoiseau puts it, books that make up a "library of feelings" and help us to overcome the effects of domination within our own selves.[8] We could place it on the shelf next to another great volume whose intention was to contest social and medical ways of regarding deviants and to return to such people, or to offer to them, the status of subjects (rather than objects) of discourse, to make it so that their words could be heard, words that contest and refute what others say of them. I am speaking, of course, of Sartre's *Saint Genet*. No doubt there are major differences between the two volumes. In Foucault's case, the struggle he enters into against psychiatric and psychoanalytic forms of interrogation is a personal struggle; he is dealing with his own experience, and he is affirming his own voice and defending his own life. Sartre, on the other hand, is writing about someone else; he sets out, with all the empathy and enthusiasm that he has at his disposal, to analyze someone else's trajectory, and to give an account of the mechanisms of domination and the processes of self-invention that are involved in it. Yet these two books, one published in the early 1950s, the other in the early 1960s, are obviously related. (The relation between them might even be called a filiation: I like to imagine that Foucault was deeply marked by his reading of Sartre's book! How could this not have been the case?) They are linked by a common gesture.

It was only towards the end of the 1970s that I got to know Foucault's book (in 1977, I believe). I thus read it after having read Sartre's (which it seems to me I read in 1974 or 1975). Sartre's book was thus the first one that counted for me during those years in which books served as a key source of support for the work of self-reinvention and self-reformulation that I was involved in—or, more precisely, for my decision to accept what I was (and therefore, of course, to reappropriate and reformulate what the hostile ambient culture repeatedly told me I was). The decision to accept what I was, to reappropriate what was said about me, changed everything—or nearly everything. It was a decision that I came to slowly; but then, after a long period of hesitation, it became quite urgent to me: a decision not to spend my life suffering from feelings of shame or fear because I was gay. That would have been too difficult, too painful. It can nearly drive people mad (a kind of madness on which psychoanalysts thrive and which they therefore work, perhaps for this very reason, to perpetuate). I had the strength, or the luck (and who knows where it came from) to take this step at a relatively young age (I was 19 or 20), first confiding my "secret" to several friends—who, in any case, had already known or suspected it and couldn't understand why I hadn't already spoken to them about it—, and then declaring in a more theatrical and ostentatious manner that it was simply not possible for me to keep this "secret" any longer.

I might put it this way, taking my inspiration from the metaphoric floral prose of Genet: there comes a moment when, being spat upon, you turn the spit into roses; you turn the verbal attacks into a garland of flowers, into rays of light. There is, in short, a moment when shame turns into pride. This pride is political through and through because it defies the deepest workings of normality and of normativity. You don't start from scratch when you set out to reformulate what you are. It is a slow and painstaking process through which you shape an identity, starting from the one imposed upon you by the social order. This is why you never completely free yourself from insult or from shame. After all, the world is constantly issuing calls to order, reactivating feelings we might prefer to forget, feelings we sometimes believe we have forgotten. If Genet's character Divine, in *Our Lady of the Flowers*, having moved beyond the crushing sense of shame she felt during her childhood and adolescence, and having transformed herself into a flamboyant figure within the queer culture of Montmartre, finds herself once again blushing when someone insults her, it is because it is impossible to ignore the social forces that surround and assail her, the forces of the norm. It is just as impossible to ignore the affects that such forces have inscribed—and are continually reinscribing—at the deepest levels of the psyches of stigmatized individuals. We all know this, all of us who experience these kinds of things in the most ordinary situations, when we find ourselves suddenly hit and bruised without expecting it, when we thought we had some kind of immunity. It is never enough, using Goffman's way of speaking, to have turned the stigma around, to have reappropriated the insult and changed its meaning; to do so does not do away with its capacity to hurt us. We walk a tightrope between the wounding meaning contained within an insulting word and the prideful reappropriation we might have made of it. We are never fully free, never completely emancipated from it. We more or less free ourselves from the burden that the social order and its subjugating force press upon us all at every moment. If shame is, in Eve Kosofsky Sedgwick's wonderful expression, a "transformational energy,"[9] we should note that self-transformation never happens without the integration of traces from the past. It preserves the past, simply because that past is the world in which we were socialized and it remains within us to a considerable extent, just as it continues to surround us within the world in which we go on living. Our past is still there in our present. So we remake ourselves, we recreate ourselves (a task that is never finished, always needing to be taken up again), but we do not make ourselves, we do not create ourselves.

It would thus be futile to set up an opposition between change or agency on the one hand and determinisms or the self-reproducing energy of the social order and of sexual norms on the other—or between ways of thinking about "freedom" and ways of thinking about "reproduction." These dimensions are inextricably bound together; they exist in an imbricated relation with each other. To take determinisms into account is not the same as affirming that nothing can change. But the effects of heretical activity, activity that calls orthodoxy and its repetitions into question will necessarily be limited and relative. Absolute "subversion" exists no more than does absolute "emancipation." Something is subverted at a particular moment; something gets slightly displaced; you push something aside; you take a step in a different direction. To put it in Foucauldian terms, we should not be dreaming of some kind of impossible "emancipation." Our best hope will be to breach certain frontiers that history has put into place and that hem in our existence.

This observation of Sartre's from his book on Genet was key for me: "What is important is not what people make of us but what we ourselves make of what they have made of us." It soon became the principle of my existence, the principle of an ascesis, the project of remaking my self.

Yet it was a double meaning that Sartre's sentence came to have in my life. It came to apply both in the domain of sexuality and in the domain of class, but in contradictory ways. In the former domain, it was a case of appropriating and claiming my insulted sexual being. But in the latter it was a case of uprooting myself from my origins. I could put it this way: in one case I needed to become what I was, but in the other I needed to reject what I was supposed to have been. Yet for me these two activities went hand in hand.

Basically, I had been convicted twice, socially speaking: one conviction was based on class, the other on sexuality. There is no escaping from sentences such as these. I bear the mark of both of them. Yet because they came into conflict with each other at a certain moment in my life, I was obliged to shape myself by playing one off against the other.

EPIL

EPILOGUE

1

WHATEVER I AM TODAY, it happened at the intersection of these two itineraries: I came to Paris in the hopes both of being able to live an openly gay life and of becoming an "intellectual." The first half of this project was not so hard to realize. The second, however, had led to a dead end. Once I had failed in my attempts to become a high school teacher as well as in my attempts to complete a doctoral dissertation, I found myself without a job and without any prospects. A solution presented itself thanks to resources I encountered within the gay subculture. Gay cruising does allow for a certain amount of mixing between classes. You can meet people whom otherwise there would be no way of meeting because their backgrounds are so different from yours or because your social horizons are so divergent. This mixing sometimes produces certain phenomena of solidarity and of mutual assistance that are perhaps not even directly experienced or perceived as such in the moment in which they occur, not unlike the experience of the process of "cultural transmission" that I described earlier. In the public park behind Notre Dame, a popular gay spot, I met a fellow with whom I had a brief affair. I was 25 at the time, and had basically run out of ideas of how to support myself. I was having a hard time admitting the obvious: that

I was going to have to give up the naive utopian dreams for the future that I had been indulging in ever since starting university. I was at loose ends, anxious, and unsettled. What was to become of me? One night my friend invited another of his friends over for dinner, and this friend brought his girlfriend. She worked at *Libération*, the daily newspaper founded at the beginning of the 1970s with the support of Sartre and Foucault, aligned with the spirit of the "struggles" of those years. This woman and I hit it off and we soon struck up an acquaintance. She asked me to write some articles... I was persistent and doggedly held on to the unexpected possibility that had presented itself to me. And so it happened that, little by little, I became a journalist. More precisely, I became a literary journalist. I wrote reviews of intellectual works; I conducted interviews (the first of them was with Pierre Bourdieu, about *Distinction*: I still remember it as if it were yesterday). This profession provided me with an unforeseen form of access to and way of participating in the intellectual world. It was a kind of participation I had never imagined in my teenage dreams or during my years as a student, but there were significant kinds of resemblance. I found myself having lunch with publishers and spending time in the company of authors. I quickly became friends with a number of them—close friends, in fact, with Pierre Bourdieu, with Michel Foucault... It was only a short while earlier that I had decided to abandon writing my thesis and yet, through a series of mysterious chance occurrences whose possibility arose from a complexly related mix of social necessities and risky decisions I had made, here I was spending time in the company of all the great names of contemporary thought. I didn't work for that particular newspaper for all that long. It was already in the process of turning itself into one of the principle vehicles of the conservative revolution that I have described at several different points in the course of this book. A vast offensive was being prepared in order to facilitate an organized shift to the right (a lot of organization went into this!) of the politico-intellectual field, in philosophy and the social sciences. Certain people's access to the public sphere and to the media, people in the fields of philosophy and the social sciences, was obviously one of the central and decisive stakes in this offensive. My own allegiances were too clearly linked to Bourdieu and to Foucault; I was too attached to the defense of critical thought and to the legacy of May 1968. Thus I quickly became undesirable, although fortunately not before I had had a chance to make a name for myself in the profession. The editor of a weekly magazine who had a hard time swallowing the fact that Bourdieu wouldn't give him the time of day and refused every invitation to write something for the magazine's columns became obsessed with this situation, and offered me a job as a way of solving it. I didn't like the magazine. I never had. And what was worse, it was even more involved in the neoconservative turn than the newspaper I just left had been. I couldn't make up my mind to accept the job. ("You need some way to earn a living," Bourdieu kept telling me, in order to convince me to take it. "I'll give you an interview and then they'll leave you in peace for two years.") In any case, I didn't really have a choice. I really did have to find a way to earn my keep!

From my very first days at the *Nouvel Observateur* I felt ill at ease (to put it mildly). And yet my name would be associated with that magazine for a good number of years even though everything about me hated the place. I never really learned to accept the situation in which I found myself: once again I was out of kilter. It wasn't just that I detested the place; there were deeper roots to my feelings of aversion. A certain little clique of academics considered the literary pages of this magazine to be their private reserve. They used these pages shamelessly to advance their own agendas, attempting to impose their power and their drift towards reactionary thought on the whole politico-intellectual scene. At every turn they would fight against anything that was truly eminent and that threatened to leave them in the shadows, against anything that was leftist and intended to remain so. My presence at the magazine was a hindrance to their plans. Every article I wrote, every interview I conducted enraged them, giving rise to invective and to threats of various kinds. (Intellectual life isn't always very pretty when you look at it up close. Its reality bears little resemblance to the idealized image you might have looking in from the outside when you are trying to find a way in.) After a series of crises and of skirmishes whose brutality I found staggering, I decided there was no point in wasting any of my energy in such fruitless and exhausting struggles. From that point on, I decided that this "job" would represent nothing more than a pay check for me, and that I would use my salary in order to write books. All in all, these painful experiences turned out to have been a source of extraordinary motivation: they inspired me to branch off in a new direction; they helped me harness my energy in order to transform myself one more time.

My first aspirations as a writer were of a literary nature: I started working on two different novels, and spent a good deal of time on them in the last half of the 1980s. The first of these two projects was inspired by my friendship—and by my conversations—with Dumézil and with Foucault. I wanted to describe three generations of gay men joined by the bonds of friendship. Three eras, three lives: each marked by permanence and by change. I wrote a hundred pages, or maybe a bit more. At a certain point I got stuck, and set the pile of pages aside in a closet. I would come back from time to time to what I called "my novel," still imagining that I would finish it one day. It was not to be! When I read Alan Hollinghurst's *The Swimming-Pool Library*, a novel that bore some resemblance to my project, I was filled with admiration and I realized what a huge gulf separated my drafts from a finished work. I literally threw my pages into the trash can. My second novel was going to portray two men together, inspired by the real-life couple formed by Benjamin Britten and Peter Pears; it would have dealt with the idea of creative activity when it is anchored in a loving relationship. At the time, I had developed a passion for Britten, and especially for his operas, which were often written with Pears's voice in mind (*Peter Grimes, Billy Budd, Death in Venice*...). Was it perseverance that I lacked? Or a novelistic talent? Or, more simply, did I realize that I was merely playing some kind of a game? Driven by old ambitions I was incapable of letting go of, it seemed I was doing little more than just going through the motions. In my imagination, I was a writer, but I had no real predisposition to become one. Little by little, I broke away from these literary temptations, although I never fully forgot them. From time to time I still find myself regretting that I didn't have the patience or the determination to pursue this path.

There was a common thread to these abandoned projects: in both cases my interest was captured by gay history and gay subjectivity. It seems bizarre now that I never had the idea to compose a story about social class—one that would, for example, take as a point of departure the path followed by a child of the working classes who leaves his family behind, a story whose framework would have allowed me to reconstruct the life of two or three generations, showing what elements divide them, and what other elements nonetheless hold them together. As it was, I didn't pursue my incursions into fictional realms any further; instead, I turned to a kind of writing that had been beckoning to me for a long time, and that I had put off for too long. I began writing about intellectual life and about the history of ideas. I started with two book-length interviews, one with Georges Dumézil and the other with Claude Lévi-Strauss. My first steps were thus an extension of my activity as a journalist, but the move to book-length projects changed everything. As I was working on the first of these books, in 1986, Dumézil suggested that I write a biography of Foucault, who had died two years earlier. Dumézil was an enormous help in the early stages of that project, providing me with a good deal of information as well as many documents before he too died. For me, the biography was a way of paying homage to Foucault at a time when both his name and his work were being regularly defamed and insulted by the various neoconservative squadrons that had taken over one by one all the major public forums, which led them to believe that the whole world shared their ideology and their sense of who was anathema. They even declared that a new "paradigm" now governed the social sciences (whereas what was happening was simply that they were attempting a kind of coup de force). My biography of Foucault was an ambitious book and a contrarian one. It was also a big success. I believe that it played an important role in helping build the resistance that was just starting to reveal itself in public circles to the ideological counterrevolution that was thriving at the time. It was quickly translated and published in a good number of other countries, which meant I began receiving invitations to take part in conferences, to deliver lectures, and so on. Little by little, the world of journalism began to leave me behind, or rather I left it. I would, of course, continue to publish a few articles each year and to conduct a few interviews, but they were less and less frequent and almost all of my time was now spent working on books and participating in activities at various universities in other countries. I had changed professions. My new life brought me into contact with authors and works that were reshaping the intellectual landscape, especially in the way that they were taking up questions previously neglected as subjects of research. I very much wanted to be a part of this movement, and so began writing more theoretically inclined kinds of work. The first to appear was *Insult and the Making of the Gay Self*, followed by *Une morale du minoritaire* [A minoritarian morality].

It had taken me some time to begin thinking in my own name. It is not at all obvious that someone would feel such an activity to be a legitimate one for them, especially if all their past has not already provided this legitimation, or if it has not come from the social world, or from various institutions in it. Whatever crazy dreams I had entertained in earlier years, it was not easy for me to feel that I had the aptitude—that I was socially authorized—to write books, especially books of theory.

Dreams are one thing, but reality is another. To make the two coincide requires a certain kind of stubbornness; but even more than that, it requires the right circumstances. When I was growing up at home, there were no books. It was the opposite of what Sartre describes in *The Words*, his autobiographical text about his childhood, where his goal is to reconstruct the history of a "vocation," or even of a "mission," which is to say a kind of social predestination to become part of literary and philosophical life. I was not "summoned" in this way.[1] The act of writing was not, for me, the sign of a future calling already being foreshadowed in the games of my childhood, in youthful verbal exploits that would be performed in front of astonished adults, adults who would be amazed by my precocious linguistic abilities, exploits that would be taken as signs of what would naturally come to fruition when the time was right. Quite the opposite, in fact. Another destiny had been laid out for me: that of being obliged to constrain my desires to fit within my limited set of social possibilities. For me it was thus a great struggle—and in the first instance a struggle with myself—to be granted certain possibilities and to be accorded certain rights that other people take for granted. I had to feel my way tentatively along pathways that for more privileged individuals had seemed wide open. Sometimes I had to find different paths to follow since the preexisting ones turned out not to be open to people like me. The new status that I found myself accorded in the mid-1990s and the new international environment in which I then found myself moving, played for me, somewhat late in the game, the role that a class *habitus* or an educational trajectory through a set of prestigious institutions would have played for other people at an earlier stage in their lives.

I thus spent a lot of time traveling, in Europe, in Latin America, and especially in the United States. I gave lectures in Chicago, I spoke at conferences in New York or at Harvard, I taught at Berkeley, I spent time at Princeton…

Yale University awarded me a prize. The work I had done on intellectual history, on homosexuality, on minoritarian subjectivities, had thus led me to a place that was nearly unimaginable for someone with my class origins on the lowest rungs on the social ladder. It wasn't just that the place I now found myself in was nearly unimaginable; in fact it was a place I had had almost no chance of attaining.

2

AS PART OF THE AWARD CEREMONY for the prize from Yale, I was asked to deliver a somewhat formal lecture. When they requested that I provide a title for the lecture and a short description, I decided I would reread in a critical fashion the books that had made it possible for me to be awarded this prize and to take part in this ceremony. My idea was to think about the manner in which we retrospectively construct our pasts using the theoretical and political categories that are made available to us by the social world in which we live. I began by describing the death of my father, the day I spent with my mother going through boxes of old photos, my rediscovery, of which each photo was a reminder, of the universe I had lived in back then. After having described my childhood as the son of a worker, I posed the question as to why it had never occurred to me to think about that history, why I had never wanted to do so, why I had never taken that history as a point of departure for some project of reflection. I cited a passage from an interview with Annie Ernaux that I had found very moving: in it, she was asked about the influence Bourdieu had had on her work, and she tells of a moment when she was quite young and taking her very first steps in the world of literature, a moment at which she noted in her journal (in 1962): "I will avenge my race!" What she meant by that, she goes on to say, is that she would avenge the world from which she came, the world of the dominated. She was still unsure what form would be best suited to carrying out this project. But she adds that a few years later when she was still "caught up in the wake of 68," she made "the discovery of *The Inheritors* [a book by Bourdieu and Jean-Claude Passeron on the French educational system]." This was "a time when [she] was having some difficulties both personally and as a teacher," and her discovery of this book constituted "a secret injunction," an injunction to "dive" deeply into her memory in order to "write about the wrenching nature of upward social mobility, the shame involved, etc."

Like her, I had felt a need, within the context of a political movement and its accompanying theoretical effervescence, to "dive" into my memory and to write in order to "avenge my race." But for me the "race" had been a different one, and so the memories I chose to explore were also different. Collective movements provide individuals with the means to constitute themselves as political subjects, and in so doing, they furnish a certain set of categories for self-perception. The frames of reference that they provide for reading yourself apply both to the present and to the past. Theoretical and political schemas both precede and have an effect on the way we think about ourselves; they create the possibility for a memory that is both individual and collective: when we look back at the past in order to think about processes of domination and subjection, we do so from the point of view of contemporary politics. The same is the case when we think about the kinds of self-reformulation we have undergone, produced by projects of resistance that may have had a self-conscious element to them, or may simply have been the result of the practices that make up our daily lives. Such political frameworks of memory define to a great extent the child one was or the childhood one had.

And yet (and this is a point Halbwachs had already called our attention to), even if it is true that collective memory—the memory of the group to which one belongs or with which one identifies and therefore helps to make exist—is one of the necessary conditions for the existence of individual memory, it is also true that each individual is a member of multiple groups, either simultaneously or in succession.[2] Sometimes these groups overlap; they are always evolving and forever transforming themselves. So "collective memory" and, along with it, individual memories and the pasts of different individuals, are not only plural, they are also changeable. They are elaborated in spaces and temporalities that are multiple and heterogeneous and that it would be pointless to try to unify or to place into some kind of hierarchical structure in order to determine which ones are important and which ones are not. After all, Annie Ernaux's first book, *Cleaned Out*, published in 1974, describes not only the social world of her childhood and adolescence. It also tells of a young woman of 20 going through the traumatic experience of a clandestine abortion.[3] And when she returns much later, in *Les Années* [The years], to the moment in which she launched her writing career in order to recuperate everything that she had "repressed as shameful," everything that was becoming "worthy of rediscovery," she insists on the extent to which that kind of "memory that takes away humiliation" had laid out for her a future that was as much political as literary and intellectual. In the course of that future she would prove capable of reappropriating different stages in her life's trajectory, different dimensions that were all constitutive of her personality: "To struggle for a woman's abortion rights, to struggle against social injustice, and to understand how she became the woman she was were all one and the same thing for her."[4]

During the period of the 1960s and 1970s, when I was a student and when Marxism dominated French intellectual life, at least on the left, all other forms of "struggle" seemed "secondary"—or they might even be denounced as "petite bourgeois distractions" from the place where attention should be focused, the only "true" struggle, the only struggle worthy of interest, that of the working class. Movements that came to be labeled as "cultural" were focusing their attention on various dimensions that Marxism had set aside: gendered, sexual, and racial forms of subjectivation, among others. Because Marxism's attention was so exclusively concentrated on class oppression, these other movements were required to find other avenues for problematizing lived experience, and they often ended up to a great extent neglecting class oppression.

As we think back over the struggle that was necessary to overcome Marxism's practice of censoring or of excluding a whole set of issues that included gender and sexuality from the very field of perception of political and theoretical problems, was it inevitable that the only way to win this struggle was in turn to censor or to repress that which Marxism had accustomed us to "perceive" as the only form of domination? Was it the case that the disappearance of Marxism, or at least the way it was expunged as a hegemonic discourse on the left, was a necessary condition for the possibility of thinking politically about the mechanisms of sexual, racial, and other forms of subjection, about the production of minoritarian subjectivities? The answer is probably yes.

But why should we be obliged to choose between different struggles being fought against different kinds of domination? If it is the nature of our being that we are situated at the intersection of several collective determinations, and therefore of several "identities," of several forms of subjection, why should it be necessary to set up one of them rather than another as the central focus of political preoccupation—even if we are aware that any movement will have a tendency to posit the principal division of the social world specific to it as the one that must take priority? If we are shaped as political subjects by discourses and by theories, should it not be incumbent upon us to construct discourses and theories that allow us not to neglect this or that aspect, not to exclude any form of oppression, any register of domination, any form of inferiorization, any form of shame that is linked to some kind of practice of insult from the range of what is considered political, or from what can be actively addressed? Shouldn't we have theories that allow us to be ready to welcome any new movement that would want to introduce new problems into the political discussion, voices that have not yet been heard, that are somehow unexpected?[5]

This lecture at Yale represented quite an ordeal for me, by which I mean, among other things, that it constituted a key moment in a process of initiation. No sooner had I delivered the lecture than I felt compelled to return to a book project I had begun shortly after my father's death, picking up where I had left off a manuscript to which I had tentatively given the title *Returning to Reims*. It was a project I had abandoned after only a very few weeks; continuing with it had seemed utterly impossible to me. But now I began in a frenzied way to read everything I could find related to the themes involved. I understood that a project like this—to write about a "return"—could only succeed if it was mediated by, or perhaps filtered through, a wide set of cultural references: literary, theoretical, political, and so on. Such references help push your thinking along, they help you formulate what you have to say. But most importantly, they permit you to neutralize the emotional charge that might otherwise be too strong if you had to confront the "real" without the help of an intervening screen. I did promise myself that it would be only after I had finished writing my final chapter that I would read the novel by Raymond Williams, *Border Country*. Something in me warned me it might exercise too much influence over my project, and so I waited. I've just finished reading it now, as I write these final pages. Its "plot" begins when a professor from a London university learns that his father has just had a heart attack and only has a short while to live. He quickly boards a train. The story then jumps back in time and we watch all the stages in a life's itinerary slowly unfold, from a working class childhood in Wales to the moment when he returns to his family just before their impending bereavement. In between, we read of the distance that grows up between him and the world of his childhood, the unease and the shame that are the inevitable consequences of this distance, and the obligation he feels, once he has "returned," to relive in his mind his whole childhood and adolescence. At the heart of the story is, of course, his departure for university, made possible thanks to the support of his parents, who also understand that one result of all their efforts and all their sacrifices will be a separation between them and their son. On the final page of the book, the main character understands that "going back" isn't really possible. It isn't possible to tear down the barriers that the years have built up. The most one can hope for, he reflects, when one tries to bring the past and the present back in touch with each other, is some kind of reconciliation with oneself and with the world that has been left behind. He somberly states that for him, "the distance is measured," and "the feeling of exile" is "ending." He declares that "by measuring the distance, we come home."[6]

Is he right or is he wrong? I remain unable to decide. What I do know is that when I got to the end of the novel, to the moment when the son learns that his father has died, the father with whom he has just barely had the time to reestablish a relationship of affection, a relationship that had either disappeared or been forgotten, I felt tears well up in my eyes. Was I about to cry? If so, over what? Over whom? The characters in the novel? My own father? I thought of him with a sense of heartache, and regretted that I hadn't gone to see him, that I hadn't tried to understand him, that I hadn't at some point tried to talk to him again. I regretted the fact that I had allowed the violence of the social world to triumph over me, as it had triumphed over him.

A few years earlier, finding myself once again in a situation where I had no steady and reliable source of income, it had seemed logical for me to take the necessary steps to find my way into the world of the French university. My books and my teaching in universities in the United States gave me the right to knock on that door. So it happened that after a long detour, I found myself once again in those very spaces that I had had to leave at the end of the 1970s, when I lacked the social competences necessary to survive there. Now I am a professor. When I told my mother I had been offered a university position, she asked me, deeply moved by the news:

"What will you be teaching? Philosophy?"

"No, sociology."

"Sociology, what's that? Something to do with society?"

Notes

PART I

1. Claude Simon, *The Jardin des Plantes*, trans. Jordan Stump (Evanston: Northwestern University Press, 2001), 149.

2. "Think, Cefisa, think of that cruel night that for a whole people became an eternal one," from a scene in Racine's *Andromaque*. (Translator's note.)

3. "Here are fruits, flowers, leaves and branches/ And now here is my heart ....," from "Green," a poem by Paul Verlaine. (Translator's note.)

4. "Space, identical to itself, whether expanding or denying/Rolls in this tedium…" from "Quand l'ombre menaça…", a sonnet by Stéphane Mallarmé. (Translator's note.)

5. Roland Barthes, *Mourning Diary*, trans. Richard Howard (New York: Hill & Wang, 2010), 73.

6. Cf. Didier Eribon, *Insult and the Making of the Gay Self*, trans. Michael Lucey (Durham: Duke University Press, 2004), 18–23.

7. Didier Eribon, *Une morale du minoritaire: Variations sur un thème de Jean Genet* (Paris Fayard, 2001); *Hérésies: Essais sur la théorie de la sexualité* (Paris: Fayard, 2003).

8. The French expression is "transfuge de classe." (Translator's note.)

9. Paul Nizan, *Antoine Bloyé* [1933], trans. Edmund Stevens (New York: Monthly Review Press, 1973), 163.

10. Annie Ernaux, *A Man's Place*, trans. Tanya Leslie (New York: Four Walls Eight Windows, 1992); *Shame*, trans. Tanya Leslie (New York: Seven Stories, 1998); *A Woman's Story*, trans. Tanya Leslie (New York: Seven Stories, 2003).

11. James Baldwin, "Notes of a Native Son" [1955], in *Notes of a Native Son* [1964] (New York: Penguin, 1995), 98.

12. Baldwin, "Notes," 85–86.

13. James Baldwin, *Conversations*, ed. Fred L Standley and Louis H. Pratt (Jackson: University Press of Mississippi, 1989), 60.

14. Encore ça que les Boches n'auront pas!

15. See, on this subject, Virginie de Luca Barrusse, *Les Familles nombreuses: Une question démographique, un enjeu politique (1880–1940)* (Rennes: Presses universitaires de Rennes, 2008). See also Remi Lenoir, *Généalogie de la morale familiale* (Paris: Seuil, 2003).

16. See Alain Coscia-Moranne, *Reims, un laboratoire pour l'habitat. Des cités-jardins aux quartiers-jardins* (Reims: CRDP Champagne-Ardenne, 2005) and Delphine Henry, *Chemin vert. L'oeuvre d'éducation populaire dans une cité-jardin emblématique, Reims 1919–1939* (Reims: CRDP Champagne-Ardenne, 2002).

17. Gilles Deleuze, "Gauche," in *Gilles Deleuze From A to Z*, DVD (Los Angeles: Semiotext(e), 2011).

18. On this working class way of dividing the world up into "us" and "them," see Richard Hoggart, *The Uses of Literacy: Aspects of Working Class Life* [1957] (New Brunswick: Transaction, 1998), 72ff.

19. See Francine Muel-Dreyfus, *Le Métier d'éducateur* (Paris: Minuit, 1983), 46–47.

20. Annie Ernaux, *A Woman's Story*, 22.

PART II

1. Perhaps this explains why supple and shifting kinds of morality can exist alongside rigid moralism in working class contexts. It is this mix of malleability in practice and ideological strictness that makes people incredibly sensitive to gossip, rumor, and to worrying over what others will say.

2. Paul Éluard, "Comprenne qui voudra," in *Au rendez-vous allemand* (Paris: Minuit, 1945). [Translator's note: an incomplete translation by George Dillon of this poem, "Understand who will," was published in *Poetry* in October 1945. Dillon seems to have left out the line "Découronnée défigurée" ("Uncrowned disfigured"). Otherwise I have cited his translation.]

3. Marguerite Duras, *Hiroshima mon amour*, trans. Richard Seaver (New York: Grove Press, 1961), 12, 59, 99.

4. Cf. Fabrice Virgili, *La France « virile ». Des femmes tondues à la Libération* (Paris: Payot, 2000).

5. Stanley Cavell, *Pursuits of Happiness: The Hollywood Comedy of Remarriage* (Cambridge, Massachusetts: Harvard University Press, 1981), 239, 263.

6. Annie Ernaux, *A Woman's Story*, 52–53.

7. I can refer the reader here to the wonderful account Carolyn Kay Steedman gives of her mother in *Landscape For a Good Woman: A Story of Two Lives* (New Brunswick, NJ: Rutgers University Press, 1987), 809. See also the harsh critique she offers (pp. 11–12) of Richard Hoggart's book, *The Uses of Literacy*, for presenting an ahistorical vision of the working class, and for celebrating its simplicity and its psychological fixity, as if the working class had simply ceased to evolve on the day that this future sociologist left it behind.

8. I've provided an analysis of this Lacanian discourse on the "causes" of homosexuality—homophobic down to its root—in *Une morale du minoritaire: Variations sur un thème de Jean Genet* (Paris: Fayard, 2001), 235–284.

9. Raymond Aron, "Science et conscience de la société," in *Les Sociétés modernes* (Paris: PUF-Quadrige, 2006), 57. [Translator's note: Eribon's book on the conservative revolution is called *D'une révolution conservatrice et de ses effets sur la gauche française* (Paris: Léo Scheer, 2007).]

10. Richard Hoggart, *A Local Habitation: Life and Times, 1918–1940* (London: Chatto & Windus, 1988).

11. John Edgar Wideman, *Brothers and Keepers* [1984] (New York: Houghton Mifflin, 2005), 26–27.

12. Wideman, *Brothers and Keepers*, 27.

13. John Edgar Wideman, *Fanon* (New York: Houghton Mifflin, 2008), 50.

14. Wideman, *Fanon*, 62–63.

15. Pierre Bourdieu, *An Invitation to Reflexive Sociology* (Chicago: University of Chicago Press, 1992),102.

16. Pierre Bourdieu, "L'idéologie jacobine" [1966], in *Interventions: Science sociale et action politique, 1961–2001* (Marseille: Agone, 2002), 56.

PART III

1. Cf. Stéphane Beaud and Michel Pialoux, *Retour sur la condition ouvrière: enquête aux usines Peugeot de Sochaux-Montbéliard* (Paris: Fayard, 1999).

2. The fact that a concept as inept as it is reactionary, that of "mass individualism," has thrived in various analyses of the "precarization" of the labor market can teach us a lot more about the sorry itinerary followed by certain sociologists who use it, leading them from a critical position on the left towards the sanctums of technocrats and neoconservative thinkers, than it can about the reality of any "transformation of the social question."

3. On the transformation in economic discourses and policies, see Frédéric Lebaron, *Le Savant, la politique et la mondialisation* (Bellecombe-en-Bauge: Le Croquant, 2003).

4. This odd formulation was her way of saying that she had voted for Le Pen in the first round of the Presidential elections of 2002, but for Chirac against Le Pen in the second round. In 2007, she voted for Sarkozy in both rounds.

5. For more on these questions, see my book *D'une révolution conservatrice et de ses effets sur la gauche française* (Paris: Léo Scheer, 2007).

6. See Jean-Paul Sartre, "Elections: A Trap for Fools," in *Life/Situations: Essays Written and Spoken*, trans. Paul Auster and Lydia Davis (New York: Pantheon, 1977), 198–210.

7. Maurice Merleau-Ponty, "On Abstaining," in *Signs*, trans. Richard C. McCleary (Evanston: Northwestern University Press, 1964), 319–20 (translation modified).

8. On the social, political, and ideological processes that led to a similar result in Great Britain—the formation of historic blocs uniting the bourgeoisie with

large segments of the popular classes in a vote for parties on the right—see Stuart Hall, *The Hard Road to Renewal: Thatcherism and the Crisis of the Left* (London: Verso, 1988).

9. On the vote for the National Front, see the article by Patrick Lehingue, "L'objectivation statistique des électorats: que savons-nous des électeurs du Front national?", in Jacques Lagroye, *La Politisation* (Paris: Belin, 2003), 247–278.

10. On the shifts from one generation to the next within the popular classes as regards their relation to the left and to the right, see the article mentioned earlier by Patrick Lehingue.

11. A quite realistic description of this French working class racism and of the living conditions of immigrant workers in the 1950s can be found in the 1967 novel by Claire Etcherelli, *Elise; or, The Real Life*, trans. June P. Wilson and Walter Benn Michaels (New York: Morrow, 1969).

12. On racism and anti-Semitism within the popular classes in France (and especially on the left), as well as on right-wing workers movements, see Zeev Sternhell, *La Droite révolutionnaire, 1885–1914* (Paris: Fayard, 2000), especially chapter 4, "L'antisémitisme de gauche," and chapter 6, "Une droite prolétarienne: les Jaunes." See also Sternhell's *Neither Right Nor Left: Fascist Ideology in France*, trans. David Maisel (Berkeley: University of California Press, 1986).

13. On theories that opposed both the left and Marxism and offered other frameworks for thinking about the social conditions of workers, their place, and the social role they play, see Sternhell, *La Droite révolutionnaire*, especially chapter 9, "À la recherche d'une assise populaire: l'Action française et le prolétariat."

14. For a critique of "experience" used as immediate "evidence," and for an analysis of the role of political discourses and theories in the sorting out of perceptions and practices and of the meanings they take on, see Joan W. Scott, "The Evidence of Experience," *Critical Inquiry* 17, no. 4 (1991): 773–797.

15. See on this point the crucial remarks made by Stuart Hall in *The Hard Road to Renewal*.

16. For an example of someone celebrating "competence" that is held in common and the "drawing of lots" as the regulatory principle of a "power of the people," see Jacques Rancière, *Hatred of Democracy*, trans. Steve Corcoran (London: Verso, 2006). Rancière seems to be vaguely aware of the problem I am discussing without ever explicitly formulating it. (Indeed, how could he without calling into

question some of his most basic ideological assumptions?) All the examples he provides of democratic forms of expression have to do with what he calls "struggles" or "movements," which is to say collective and organized manifestations of dissident opinion. This reveals that the "power of the people" as a foundation of democracy is never that of undifferentiated and interchangeable individuals. It is always already inscribed in heterogeneous social and political frameworks that are in conflict with each other. So it is rather these very frameworks themselves that any reflection on democracy should place at the heart of its preoccupations and interrogations.

17. This crucial element—the mediation of political parties—is almost entirely absent from Sartre's model or is dismissed by him. (When he wrote his article on elections, he was caught up in a belief in a political revolution that would arise from spontaneous action.) But it is emphasized by Bourdieu in his article "Le mystère du ministère: Des volontés particulières à la 'volonté générale,'" *Actes de la recherche en sciences sociales* 140 (2001): 7–13.

18. Here I am in agreement with the analysis of Stuart Hall in "Gramsci and Us," in *The Hard Road to Renewal*, 163–173.

19. They are aided in this, of course, by the intellectuals of the party and of the government, who work to delimit what counts as political and what doesn't, what is "democratic" and what is "anti-democratic," and so on. This kind of work represents the opposite of what intellectual work should be—to think about the shifting nature of the social world rather than to seek to prescribe what that world is—, and also the opposite of a democratic kind of activity, which cannot be imprisoned in the diktats of authoritarian ideologues such as these, tied to all the technocracies and bureaucracies that are out there, tied to institutions and the powers that be. As a salutary antidote to these antidemocratic impulses, see Sandra Laugier, *Une autre pensée politique américaine: la démocratie radicale d'Emerson à Stanley* Cavell (Paris: Michel Houdiard, 2004).

PART IV

1. Pierre Bourdieu, *Sketch for a Self-Analysis*, trans. Richard Nice (Chicago: University of Chicago Press, 2008), 94–96.

2. Bourdieu, *Sketch*, 94.

3. Bourdieu, *Sketch*, 99–100.

4, On the link between the masculinist values of boys from the popular or working classes (notable in their rejection of authority, and their hostility towards good students, whom they take to be conformist) and their exclusion from the educational system, see Paul Willis, *Learning to Labour: How Working Class Kids Get Working Class Jobs* (Westmead: Saxon House, 1977).

5. See Bourdieu, *Sketch*, 79–82. I recounted in my journal for the year 2004—the year in which this book appeared in France—a number of the conversations I had with him on this subject and others while he was working on the manuscript and had given it to me to read. (See Didier Eribon, *Sur cet instant fragile ... Carnets, janvier-août 2004* [Paris: Fayard, 2004].) In reply to my criticisms, he said that when he returned to working on the book, for the French publication that would happen after it had appeared in Germany, he would endeavor to modify these pages. It was something he wasn't given the time to do.

6. On the masculinist—and also class-based—categories that are at work in the discourse by which sociology constructs itself as a "science" in opposition to philosophy, see Geoffroy de Lagasnerie, "L'inconscient sociologique: Émile Durkheim, Claude Lévi-Strauss et Pierre Bourdieu au miroir de la philosophie," *Les Temps modernes* 654 (2009): 99–108.

7. This is a point I developed in *Insult and the Making of the Gay Self* and *Une morale du minoritaire*. This specifically gay use of culture is missing from the model Bourdieu proposes in *Distinction: A Social Critique of the Judgement of Taste*, trans. Richard Nice (Cambridge, Massachusetts: Harvard University Press, 1984). When I made this remark to Bourdieu one day, he immediately agreed with me.

8. Richard Hoggart points this out clearly in *A Local Habitation*.

9. See Bourdieu, *Distinction*, 125–168.

10. Paul Nizan, *The Watchdogs: Philosophers of the Established Order* [1932], trans. Paul Fittingoff (New York: Monthly Review Press, 1971).

PART V

1. Guy Hocquenghem would offer a severe critique of Reich in *Homosexual Desire*, trans. Daniella Dangoor (Durham: Duke University Press, 1993), first published in 1972. On the infatuation of certain segments of the gay movement of the 1970s with Reich, see Thierry Voeltzel, *Vingt ans et après* (Paris: Grasset, 1978), especially pages 18 and 29. This book is a conversation between a young

man, age 20, and an "older friend" who is, in fact, Michel Foucault. I discussed this volume in *Insult and the Making of the Gay Self*, pp. 303–309.

2. See Michel Foucault, *The History of Sexuality, Volume 1: An Introduction*. [La Volonté de savoir], trans. Robert Hurley (New York: Vintage, 1990). For more on this point see my discussion of Foucault's project in the third part of *Insult and the Making of the Gay Self*, in *Une morale du minoritaire*, and in *Échapper à la psychanalyse* (Paris: Léo Scheer, 2005).

3. See Eve Kosofsky Sedgwick, *Epistemology of the Closet* (Berkeley: University of California Press, 1990). Her book was a great source of inspiration to me as I wrote *Insult and the Making of the Gay Self*.

4. [Translator's note: The French examples given are "Quelle heure est-elle?", and "Quel temps fait-elle?", feminized forms of the traditional expressions for asking the time or asking about the weather.]

5. George Chauncey, *Gay New York: Gender, Urban Culture, and the Making of the Gay Male World, 1890–1940* (New York: Knopf, 1994).

6. Erving Goffman, *Stigma: Notes on the Management of Spoiled Identity* (Englewood Cliff, NJ: Prentice-Hall, 1963). On symbolic domination, see Pierre Bourdieu, *Pascalian Meditations*, trans. Richard Nice (Stanford: Stanford University Press, 2000), 169–71.

7. Cf. Georges Dumézil, *Loki* (Paris: Maisonneuve, 1948), and my comments on this book in "Le crime de Loki," in *Hérésies*, 19–32.

8. See Patrick Chamoiseau, *Écrire en pays dominé* (Paris: Gallimard, 1997), 23–24. Chamoiseau coins the word *sentimenthèque* to describe this kind of collection of volumes that speak to our feelings.

9. Eve Kosofsky Sedgwick, "Shame, Theatricality, and Queer Performativity: Henry James's *The Art of the Novel*," in *Touching Feeling: Affect, Pedagogy, Performativity* (Durham: Duke University Press, 2002), 35–65.

EPILOGUE

1. Jean-Paul Sartre, *The Words*, trans. Bernard Frechtman (New York: Vintage, 1981), 169–70.

2. See Maurice Halbwachs, *On Collective Memory*, trans. Lewis A. Coser (Chicago: University of Chicago Press, 1992), and *The Collective Memory*, trans. Francis J. Ditter, Jr. and Vida Yazdi Ditter (New York: Harper & Row, 1980).

3. Annie Ernaux, *Cleaned Out* [*Les Armoires vides*], trans. Carol Sanders (Elmwood Park, IL: Dalkey Archive Press, 1990).

4. Annie Ernaux, *Les Années* (Paris: Gallimard, 2008), 121.

5. Didier Eribon, "The Dissenting Child: A Political Theory of the Subject," a lecture given on April 9, 2008, at the award ceremony for the James Robert Brudner Memorial Prize.

6. Raymond Williams, *Border Country* (New York: Horizon Press, 1962), 351.